POTLUCK DESSERTS

POTLUCK
DESSERTS

SIMPLE, NOSTALGIC RECIPES FROM A TRUSTED GUIDE IN THE WORLD OF QUEER BAKING.

JUSTIN BURKE credits his first queer potluck with changing his life. Gathering around a table piled high with homemade food evoked a sense of unity that bridged individuals beyond social norms, where chosen families could gather, share recipes, and connect with one another. Two decades later, that magical night continues to inspire Burke in his work merging his passion for food with his journey of self-discovery, whipping up relatable, homemade desserts that defy traditional labels and hold their own next to their avant-garde counterparts.

Now a venerated potluck pro, Burke shares his personal and professional experiences in his debut cookbook, *Potluck Desserts*, through playful, delicious recipes like Lemon-Thyme Bars, Gooey Butter Corn Cake, Chocolate Cherry Soda Cake, and more. Refined yet approachable, these stylish sweets are organized by baking dish—sheet pans, rectangular pans and foil tins, loaf pans, casserole dishes, and bowls, Bundts, and other round things—and are tagged by time to further simplify the process. Complete with charming personal anecdotes, reflections on potlucks and the queer community, and stunning photography of an abundance of good food, *Potluck Desserts* gives every home baker the tools, confidence, and pride to serve beloved, nostalgic dishes that everyone will love—colleagues, friends, families, and chosen families included.

"This book embodies what a shared table is all about . . . love, acceptance, delicious food, forming bonds, and safety. Justin Burke beautifully brings us on the journey of his life and the delicious discovery for baking along the way. Each recipe is more than just something to eat, but they represent what happens when people gather together in love and celebration."

—BRIAN HART HOFFMAN,
founder and editor-in-chief at *Bake from Scratch*

"*Potluck Desserts* is truly a brilliant cookbook. . . . Justin Burke injects pops of color and bold flavor into beloved classics like icebox cakes, fluff salads, and ambrosia. Boxed mixes? They're no longer collecting dust—they're stepping up as key players in these reinvented favorites! I'm counting down the days to my next potluck, ready to indulge in spoonfuls of gooey butter corn cake."

—JEREMY SALAMON, chef/owner of Agi's Counter

JUSTIN BURKE

PHOTOGRAPHY BY Brian Samuels

JOYFUL RECIPES TO SHARE WITH PRIDE

Countryman Press
An Imprint of W. W. Norton & Company
Independent Publishers Since 1923

Printed in China
First Edition

For information about special discounts for bulk purchases, please contact W. W. Norton Special Sales at specialsales@wwnorton.com or 800-233-4830

Manufacturing through Asia Pacific Offset
Book design by Allison Chi
Production manager: Devon Zahn

Countryman Press
www.countrymanpress.com

An imprint of W. W. Norton & Company, Inc.
500 Fifth Avenue, New York, NY 10110
www.wwnorton.com

978-1-68268-824-3

1 2 3 4 5 6 7 8 9 0

To Jasper,

With all my love, may you always feel the embrace of your blood and chosen families. As you venture into the world, I hope you build a chosen family not out of necessity but as a reflection of your vibrant spirit and the connections you forge.

Love,
Pop

CONTENTS

INTRODUCTION

Twenty-three years ago, I could never have imagined where life would lead me today. None of the dreams or fantasies I concocted to escape my reality as a kid hinted at a future in food or in embracing my identity as a queer, nonbinary person. Nor the opportunity to bring the two together and write about it professionally. Yet, here I am, reflecting on a path that seems so clear in hindsight. My journey wasn't a well-crafted plan but rather came from a willingness to embrace discomfort, to open myself up to others, and to listen actively. Essentially, it was about embodying the nature of life outside societal norms. Trust me, it hasn't been easy. But I prefer celebrating queer joy over the traumas society often imposes on our community.

Immediately after graduating high school in 2002, I impulsively moved from my small desert town in Southern California to Orange County. At that young age, I didn't worry about where I'd live, finding a job, or even how I'd sustain myself. I picked up and left, believing that anything would be better than the life I had known for the past 18 years. This decision was the best thing I could have done, as it liberated me from the confines of my upbringing. It taught me the importance of not navigating life alone, that each relationship is unique, and that our past experiences don't define all future connections. This lesson became especially clear after I met Javier.

Javier was the first friend I made in Orange County. We both worked at Disneyland. His vibrant presence drew me in, offering a sense of comfort I had been missing. He became my guide and support, showing me what living openly in the LGBTQIA+ community meant. In return, Javier recognized my potential. After a month of friendship and allowing him to see the real me, he invited me to my first queer potluck—an event that would change my life forever.

The evening of the potluck at Javier's Long Beach apartment was magical. The Southern California sunset painted the sky in warm hues as I stood outside, contemplating a pivotal moment. Would I finally accept and love myself for who I am?

With a mix of anxiety and determination, I made my way inside, carrying Shirley's Cake (page 51), a cherished family recipe. Javier greeted me with open arms and a wide grin, ushering me into an apartment filled with laughter, music, and the aroma of unfamiliar food. It wasn't just a gathering but a scene from *Tales of the City*.

Hand in hand, Javier guided me through the crowd, where conversations buzzed with stories of dreams and struggles. The potluck table symbolized unity, bridging individuals beyond societal norms. Amidst the laughter, I felt a sense of belonging.

Leaving Javier's apartment that night, I realized that potlucks create chosen families. Two decades later, that transformative night continues to inspire me, shaping my career as a pastry chef, food writer, and now, the author of *Potluck Desserts*.

My Long Beach chosen family has been a constant source of strength, guiding me through life's challenges. Although I only remained in Orange County for three months after that night, the experiences and connections I forged there altered the course of my life, providing me with a sense of belonging in a fragmented world. This then led me, after a decade as a pastry chef and food writer, to my niche exploring the intersection of food and the queer community, just as the term *queer food* began to gain traction. I vividly recall reading John Birdsall's words, perhaps in the food magazine *Lucky Peach*, urging me to merge my passion for food with my queerness and to live authentically.

Yes, this cookbook contains recipes, but it's also a celebration of connections within the queer community. The 75 dessert recipes are intertwined with stories of my chosen and biological families, each one representing a pivotal moment in my journey of self-discovery. As you flip through these pages, you'll find desserts that defy traditional labels, like Whole Wheat Chocolate Chip Cookie Bars with Salted Vanilla Frosting (page 88), which is a recipe that embodies my rebellion against conformity.

In a rare twist of fate, as I started my career as a pastry chef, my professional journey mirrored my personal one, navigating against societal restraints and expectations. Despite the media's portrayal of success and full communal support, the Boston chef community didn't welcome me with open arms. I entered the food scene at a time when chefs were transforming into celebrities, and cuisine was becoming a showcase of classically trained skill, ingredient manipulation, and appropriation. As a self-taught baker fond of nostalgic home baking, I was determined to bring back comfort and familiarity to dessert menus. However, I was often treated as a fraud within the industry. Despite these challenges, I remained steadfast, believing that relatable, homey desserts deserved a place alongside their avant-garde counterparts. Moreover, as a queer person in professional kitchens, I was focused on breaking barriers and I refused to compromise my identity for the sake of a fictitious successful career.

Potluck Desserts is a celebration of the queer narrative and our journey of finding ourselves and forging chosen families. It highlights where our history has been captured all these years, blended with the stories of recipes and communal bonds shared and passed down. Just as important, these recipes are also connected to my queer story, where I found the strength to survive and thrive and, for example, found the confidence to layer a malt-infused whipped cream on top of a cream cheese–Cool Whip layer for a Malt Chocolate Delight (page 171).

This is not just a cookbook to instruct; it's a journey. It explores flavors and skills; every recipe is a chapter in the story of strangers becoming friends and friends becoming family. This book is a warm celebration meant to uplift you, a torchbearer for your own story in a world where many stories go unheard.

WHY QUEER POTLUCKS?

I need to address the elephant in the room before moving on. Let's unpack this whole "queer potluck" thing before we dive in. To understand why potlucks are important to the LGBTQIA+ community, it's important to understand how food, better known as queer food, plays a pivotal role in our community. I know some folks might be scratching their heads, wondering, "What the heck is queer about food?" Well, brace yourselves because queer food is a legit thing, and yes, we queers throw potlucks.

First, forget the over-the-top stereotypes, especially the ones tied to parties hosted by gay men. We're not talking fancy china and bougie wine here. Quite the opposite—the queer potlucks I'm talking about are all about chill vibes, not flashy glam.

Javier's potluck was held at his home. The apartment wasn't a swanky penthouse, but it was near the coast and a breeze made the linen curtains dance. The lighting? Hand-me-down lamps. The furniture? Shades of olive green, burnt orange, and tan. Throw blankets covered the well-loved pieces, and the dining table, worn from years of use, sported a plaid tablecloth that felt more like a giant doily. Forget about avant-garde aesthetics, this gathering oozed simplicity and comfort.

That night's food came in foil pans, thrifted Pyrex, and yard sale dishware. We used paper plates and Solo cups. The drinks were sourced from a nearby gas station. The background music came from a 6-disc CD player spinning burned CDs, everything from the latest hits to '90s bangers, set to a volume that allowed for easy conversations, interrupted by the occasional burst of dancing when a favorite track played.

The genuine connections and the freedom to be yourself without judgment is the essence of a queer potluck—a mix of real presence, total acceptance, and unapologetic transparency.

Now, you might be wondering why are queer potlucks such a big deal? Before we get into that, let's make one thing clear: Potlucks aren't just for the LGBTQIA+ community. I'm not claiming we invented them, but our potlucks have a unique history of resilience, community building, and resistance.

In times when mainstream society tried to erase us, we found strength behind the scenes, sharing meals and stories. A place to build community and resist being silenced.

The roots of potlucks go beyond the LGBTQIA+ spectrum, reaching various cultures worldwide. They're called different things—covered dish suppers, Jacob's joins, buffet communautaire, bring-a-plate—but they all bring people together to share a meal and find sanctuary in each other.

The term *potluck* itself goes back to

16th-century England, combining *pot* and *luck*, emphasizing the chance you take with whatever's in the pot. These gatherings embody embracing the unknown, coming together vulnerably, and finding joy in the unpredictable mix of dishes and stories.

Now, food in queer communities is more than just sustenance; it's a way to forge relationships, create safe spaces, create a platform for activism, and collect our narratives. Queer food isn't just about the dish; it's the pieces of the whole experience that a meal weaves together.

The Queer Food Movement, a silent force for decades, is gaining recognition. It's about the exchange of a meal and how it makes you feel, tying your experience into the narrative of queer culture and history.

Queer potlucks, with their laid-back charm, have become a sanctuary for unconditional acceptance, a space for chosen family-making. In a world that sometimes doesn't get us, these gatherings become a refuge where we can be ourselves, share stories, and savor the richness of life.

GAB 'N' JAVA

IF IT WEREN'T for two pioneers, **Del Martin** and **Phyllis Lyon**, this cookbook about the blend of potluck-style desserts and the legacy of queer potlucks wouldn't exist. In the 1950s, living in San Francisco, they noticed a lack of safe spaces for lesbians, compared to their gay counterparts. With the era's rampant homophobia and violence against women, finding a safe haven was crucial but challenging. Undeterred, Martin and Lyon took matters into their own hands and created a safe space. Their first gathering, a dinner among four couples in September 1955, was the start of something much bigger. Within five years, chapters of the Daughters of Bilitis, as they called themselves, had sprung up across the country.

As the organization grew, so did the concept of gathering around food within the gay community and beyond. In rural and suburban areas, far from the bustling city scenes, gay men began hosting secret gatherings to build community and safe spaces. These potluck-style events were happening nationwide, coinciding with increased political activism within the LGBTQIA+ community. The community's voice grew stronger with each new generation, and the movement gained momentum.

Martin and Lyon's efforts not only provided a safe space for LGBTQIA+ individuals but also contributed to the broader LGBTQIA+ movement. Their gatherings nurtured, bonded, and built chosen families, invigorating and amplifying queer voices.

HOW TO USE THIS BOOK

In the early days of my career in professional kitchens, I was made to believe that desserts needed to be overly complex, with convoluted ingredients and pretentious names. I desperately wanted to succeed, fit in, and be taken seriously. So I altered my approach and tried to "pass" as a trained pastry chef. However, I felt like a liar with each dish, losing touch with the essence of baking that initially drew me in. I knew there was a place for nostalgic, homey desserts on restaurant menus and that my style of baking was just as valid.

Over time, I adopted a different approach. I began to integrate new ingredients and skills into my recipes thoughtfully, preserving the integrity of the original recipe. Studying classic culinary techniques at home allowed me to draw parallels to home baking and apply that approach in professional kitchens. I taught myself to identify restaurant lingo, like *crémeux*, which is a pudding with whipped cream folded in to decrease density, and I developed a language that enabled me to communicate adjustments with authenticity and clarity, ultimately carving out my identity in the kitchen. This journey instilled in me the confidence to create desserts that were both true to myself and immensely satisfying, demonstrating that baking could be both an art and a science—demanding precision while rewarding creativity and intuition.

This journey of self-discovery led me to a profound realization: The most essential ingredient in any recipe is not some spice found on Amazon, or a trending fruit, but the love and care invested in its creation. It's about taking simple, humble ingredients—flour, sugar, butter, eggs—and transforming them into something extraordinary that brings joy to the baker and those who taste it.

The recipes in this book are not instructions to be followed mechanically; they're an invitation for you to find your voice in the kitchen, to experiment, explore, take risks, and discover new flavors and textures. They celebrate the simple pleasure of baking and the joy of sharing something special with loved ones.

These desserts may appear unassuming, but they are far from ordinary. They are not "lazy" or "basic"—as with all quality homemade dishes, making them invites creativity and requires some skill. And I've organized the recipes by the vessels they're baked in, making it easier for you to choose based on your mood and occasion.

This book champions authenticity and calls for the use of tools and ingredients accessible to all. Regardless of your schedule, whether you're a novice or an experienced baker, I hope you'll find confidence and pride in your creations. I believe that baking should be accessible to everyone, and so I've ensured that all the ingredients can be found in any supermarket. Additionally, I've included some recipes that utilize boxed mixes, which are customized to enhance flavor or purpose.

So when you start baking from this book, do what I do. Take a deep breath, remember you're baking for the joy and love of it, and for someone—and enjoy the experience and be proud.

The Chapters

RECTANGULAR AND SQUARE PANS (AND DISPOSABLE TINS): These versatile vessels are perfect for various baked goods, such as brownies, cakes, confections, and bars. More important, they can be easily transported in the vessel they're baked in without hassle, and upon arrival you can choose to serve straight from the pan or transfer to a platter. Suppose you're worried about losing your beloved pan at a potluck. In that case, disposable tins come to the rescue. They are available in almost every size, similar to their sturdy counterparts. If you can, save that disposable tin and reuse it later on.

SHEET PANS: Often associated solely with cookies or jelly rolls, these pans have many more uses for baking desserts, such as bars, cakes, pies, and tarts. They expedite baking for a crowd, as they allow you to bake everything on one pan. That, in turn, makes it easier for you to portion and transfer to a platter or to score portions and leave them on the pan for guests to serve themselves. Sizes to have are the half sheet (13½-by-18½-inch) and quarter sheet (9½-by-13½-inch) pans.

LOAF PANS: In addition to quick bread, both smaller cakes and no-bake desserts can be made in a loaf pan. This pan is a great choice when refrigerator space is tight.

CASSEROLE DISHES (AKA BAKING DISHES): These deep-dish, oven-safe vessels offer versatility for creating layered desserts, serving saucy treats, or allowing guests to scoop their portions directly onto their plates. These dishes are quintessential to home baking and are my preferred choice when baking for potlucks.

BOWLS, BUNDTS, AND OTHER ROUND THINGS: This category is free-for-all and encompasses everything circular. These vessels are perfect for dessert salads, trifles, and Bundts, as well as cakes and pies.

Timing

Like you, I select recipes based on the time they require. Sometimes, you're looking for a quick fix; other times, you're ready for a long, leisurely bake; occasionally, you're planning ahead. I've labeled recipes with a timing

indicator to simplify the guessing game. You won't find yourself 30 minutes in only to realize the recipe calls for an overnight rest.

THIRTY MINUTES OR LESS: It's self-explanatory, but these recipes take about 30 minutes from start to finish.

AN HOUR OR SO: Most of the recipes in this book typically require 45 minutes to 2 hours. This isn't because you'll be actively baking for that entire duration, but instead will be waiting for one step to finish before progressing to the next.

BETTER MADE THE NIGHT BEFORE: These recipes require anywhere from 30 minutes to an hour or more to make, but include resting overnight. There have been times when I've made desserts, tasted them within an hour of baking, and thought they were terrible. Instead of tossing them out, I popped them in the refrigerator while considering what to do. To my surprise, the next day, they were incredible. These recipes benefit from rest and cooling down, allowing the flavors to settle and marry. Other desserts in this chapter need to firm up overnight before slicing into them.

HOW I BAKE AT HOME: A FEW METHODS I PREFER

Like any home baker, I have my own preferred methods that I use regularly. These methods are a preference, not a necessity, to successfully make these recipes. However, it's important to understand why I use them. Many of these techniques I learned in professional kitchens, and I adapted them for when I'm baking at home for pleasure rather than for work.

Line Pans with Parchment Paper

I err on the side of caution when I bake and always line my pans with parchment paper. Is it absolutely necessary? Not really, as long as you grease your pans generously with butter or baking spray. I use parchment paper for two main reasons:

1. Leaving an overhang on two sides of the pan makes it easy to lift out the bake and slice it into portions without struggling with the edges of the pan.
2. I'm not always sure if the gathering I'm attending will serve directly from the pans. Some hosts prefer transferring items to a platter or tray, and this transfer is much easier to do with a parchment-lined bake.

In these recipes, I include my method: grease the pan, line it with parchment paper, and then lightly grease the paper. However, if you know you'll be serving directly from the pan or simply don't have parchment paper, rest assured that this step is optional and won't compromise the final bake.

Cake Flour for One-Layer Cakes

I like to use cake flour or half cake flour and half all-purpose flour to make one-layer cakes. I do this to create a more delicate crumb and lighter cake (thanks to the lower protein levels of cake flour). The cake recipes in this book are all one-layer, so you'll see cake flour used often. But if you don't have cake flour or prefer not to use it, you can make a version of your own using all-purpose flour and cornstarch.

1. For every cup of cake flour required, measure 1 cup of all-purpose flour.
2. Remove 2 tablespoons of the all-purpose flour from the cup.
3. Replace the removed all-purpose flour with 2 tablespoons of cornstarch.
4. Sift or whisk the all-purpose flour and cornstarch together to thoroughly combine them.

This version will help lower the protein content of the all-purpose flour, mimicking store-bought cake flour.

Use Vanilla Bean Paste When You Can

Vanilla bean paste is the only chef-y ingredient I always keep on hand. I prefer paste over vanilla bean pods because it yields the same benefits as fresh vanilla and lasts longer, which saves money. Plus, the paste can be substituted for vanilla extract 1:1 when you want a more vibrant, bold flavor and its bean specks to show. If you don't have vanilla bean paste, use vanilla extract instead. It'll still taste great!

No Scale Necessary; Volume Measurements Will Work

What I'm about to say might be controversial to some, but for home baking—unless you're making bread, laminated doughs like croissants and puff pastry, chiffon and sponge cakes, or custards that require precise measurements—you don't need a scale for weight measurements. Volume measurements (cups, spoons, and similar tools) work just as well. With this in mind, the recipes in this book can all be made with volume measurements, but I've also provided weight quantities for those who prefer using a scale.

If you're using volume measurements, it's important to note my methods. When measuring flour, to avoid compacting I spoon the flour into the measuring cup rather than scooping the cup into the flour.

When measuring light and dark brown sugars, I lightly pack them. For powdered sugar, I sift it first to eliminate any clumps and then spoon it into the measuring cup.

IN THE PANTRY AND IN THE CABINETS

The Pantry

I hate grocery shopping. Not many people know this, but I've felt this way since childhood, and it persists despite my career in food. Grocery shopping for ingredients overwhelms me with endless possibilities. My overactive mind can't help but bounce ideas for what I could make. I tend to spiral. To solve this, I always have a list and stick to it. I gather what I need, and I check out quickly. This approach allows me to maintain a well-stocked pantry and refrigerator with the foundational items I need for baking. I stick to what I use regularly because those are the things that inspire me—and it encourages me to find ways to create a variety of dishes with as few ingredients as possible.

What I try to have on hand at all times:

SWEET: granulated sugar, light brown sugar, dark brown sugar, powdered sugar, light corn syrup, molasses, sorghum

SPICES: ground cinnamon, ground cardamom, ground ginger, ground nutmeg, ground clove, kosher salt

SEEDS AND NUTS: poppy seeds, sesame seeds, almonds, walnuts, pecans, cashews, macadamia nuts, pistachios

BUTTER: unsalted and salted dairy butter, creamy peanut butter, chunky peanut butter, cashew butter

OILS: vegetable, olive oil

DAIRY: whole milk, buttermilk, heavy whipping cream, half-and-half, sour cream, sweetened condensed milk, sweetened condensed coconut milk, evaporated milk

CHEESE: cream cheese, mascarpone, ricotta, cottage cheese

WHEAT: all-purpose flour, cake flour, whole wheat flour, almond flour, cornmeal, graham cracker crumbs

EXTRACTS: vanilla, almond, coconut, vanilla bean paste

CHOCOLATES: dark, semi-sweet, milk, white, mini semi-sweet chips, butterscotch chips, unsweetened cocoa powder, unsweetened Dutch-processed cocoa powder

FROZEN: Cool Whip, mixed frozen berries, frozen peaches, puff pastry

BOXED MIXES: instant chocolate pudding, instant vanilla pudding, instant white chocolate pudding, instant pistachio pudding, instant butterscotch pudding, yellow cake mix, strawberry and cherry JELL-O mix

MISCELLANEOUS: old-fashioned oats, shredded sweetened coconut

FRUIT: lemons, apples, blueberries, raspberries, oranges, limes

CANNED FRUIT: mandarin oranges, crushed pineapple, pineapple slices, maraschino cherries

DRIED FRUIT: apricots, golden raisins, freeze-dried strawberries

FRESH HERBS: thyme, mint

The Equipment

Although I can maintain a pantry and refrigerator stocked primarily with essential baking ingredients without frills, I can't resist kitchen and baking equipment. I love to collect pans, rolling pins, and old baking gadgets as art. I'll admit to having more than one stand mixer, a drawer filled with bench scrapers, cake testers, and Microplane fine graters, and a laundry room turned baking equipment storage area, complete with hooks holding more than six aprons (with another drawer upstairs filled with more), a kitchen hat, pots and pans galore, hooks inside the pantry for fine mesh sieves, and a cupboard overflowing with mixing bowls. If you were to judge my kitchen solely by its equipment, you'd quickly guess I'm a chef and food writer.

But here's the thing: I only need a few things to get the job done. In fact, I often think about how our great-great-grandparents could make cakes, pies, and loaves of bread by hand without any of these modern conveniences or gadgets that we're convinced we need to cook and bake effectively at home. When writing this book, I kept this in mind, ensuring that the recipes could be executed by hand with the essential equipment found in most homes. You will not need to purchase specialized tools.

Here are the essential tools and equipment needed for these recipes.

- Wooden spoons
- Rubber spatula
- Mixing bowls
- Measuring cups and spoons
- 2-cup (and bigger) measuring cups
- Whisk
- Electric hand mixer
- Sheet pans: 13½-by-18½-inch half sheet pan, 9½-by-13½-inch quarter sheet pan
- 9-by-13-inch pan
- 9-by-9-inch and 8-by-8-inch pans
- 9-by-5-inch loaf pan
- Rectangular and oval casserole dishes: 9-inch, 11-inch, 15-inch
- 10-inch springform pan, 10-cup Bundt pan, 10-cup tube pan
- Precut parchment paper
- Silicone baking mats
- Aluminum foil
- Disposable pans, 9-by 13-inch and 9-by-9-inch
- Fine mesh sieve
- Pots and pans
- Microplane fine grater
- Hand citrus juicer
- Scale (optional)

CHAPTER ONE

RECTANGULAR AND SQUARE PANS (AND DISPOSABLE TINS)

When it comes to potluck food, rectangular shapes dominate my thoughts, with perhaps a nod to squares for smaller portions. Something about a 9-by-13-inch pan covered in aluminum foil, the sound of crinkling as guests reveal their culinary creations, epitomizes potluck gatherings. Rectangular pans are like the mascots of these events, offering a sense of uniformity, especially when they're in disposable foil tins, all appearing identical until you're standing over the table, marveling at the unique colors, textures, and aromas of each dish. Arriving early to a potluck allows you to witness the parade of guests, each carrying similarly shaped pans wrapped in foil, creating a synchronized march of anticipation.

Before the treat is cut, only the top layer is exposed, leaving grazers to wonder what lies beneath the toasted coconut frosting or a thick layer of powdered sugar. Is it a cake? Perhaps it's something cold, or maybe it has a center filled with jam and is held together by its neighboring slices. The possibilities are endless, sparking curiosity and imagination.

I also appreciate the communal aspect of eating from rectangular and square pans, patiently waiting for the spoon or serving spatula to be passed along, or the excitement of the first person diving in to reveal the layers of a rich, soaked poke cake.

These pans are often our first introduction to baking as children, used for making fudgy brownies, buttery blondies, and simple one-layer cakes. Whether stacked precariously in bottom cabinets, aged from generational use, or appearing temporarily in our lives and serving a purpose before being discarded, these pans are integral to our culinary experiences. They have been the canvas for my earliest baking experiments, each dessert telling a story of discovery and delight as I learned to balance flavors and textures to create treats that would please a crowd. With their easy portability and straightforward presentation, these rectangular delights have been my companions in countless gatherings, where they never fail to bring smiles and satisfaction.

These bakes in same-shaped pans are where my culinary journey began, linking stories and experiences that I eagerly share at queer potlucks, connecting with like-minded individuals who appreciate the significance of these simple yet profound vessels.

BLUEBERRY POPPY SEED POKE CAKE

FOR THE CAKE

2 cups (250 g) all-purpose flour
2 teaspoons baking powder
½ teaspoon kosher salt
1 tablespoon poppy seeds
½ cup (113 g) unsalted butter, room temperature
1 cup (200 g) granulated sugar
2 eggs
1 teaspoon vanilla extract
1 cup (240 g) whole milk

FOR THE BLUEBERRY SAUCE

1 pint fresh blueberries, about 2 cups (300 g)
½ cup (105 g) granulated sugar
¼ cup (60 g) water
1 tablespoon cornstarch
Juice of 1 lemon
1 teaspoon vanilla extract

FOR THE CREAM CHEESE FROSTING

One 8-ounce package cream cheese, softened
½ cup (60 g) powdered sugar
1 teaspoon vanilla extract
1 cup (240 g) heavy whipping cream
Blueberries for garnish

When people ask me, as a pastry chef, what my favorite thing to bake is, they probably expect me to mention something fancy like laminated dough or intricate pâte à choux creations. But the truth is, I could happily spend the rest of my days making poke cakes. There's just something about their simplicity and limitless potential for creativity that speaks to me. You can turn them into anything you can dream up.

I could have easily filled an entire cookbook with poke cake recipes, but I limited myself to just two. One of my favorites is this blueberry poppy seed poke cake. It's a twist on the classic version, which usually involves pouring gelatin or sweetened condensed milk over a plain cake. Instead, this version features a fresh, vibrant blueberry sauce poured over a buttery vanilla cake with poppy seeds. The whole thing is topped with a lightly sweetened cream cheese frosting, which balances out the berries' tartness and the cake's richness. It's a flavor combination that always works.

1 Preheat your oven to 350° F and spray a 9-by-13-inch pan with baking spray. Set aside.

2 Prepare the cake. In a medium bowl, whisk together the flour, baking powder, salt, and poppy seeds until evenly combined. Set aside.

3 In a separate medium bowl with an electric hand mixer, cream the butter and sugar until light and fluffy, 2 to 3 minutes. Add the eggs and vanilla and mix until evenly combined, about 1 minute.

4. Gradually add the flour mixture to the butter-egg ingredients, alternating with the milk until evenly combined with a few visible flour streaks.

5. Pour the batter into the prepared pan and spread evenly. Bake for 20 to 30 minutes, or until light golden brown or a toothpick or cake tester insert into the middle comes out clean. Cool on a wire rack.

6. Meanwhile, prepare the blueberry sauce. In a medium saucepan over medium heat, add the blueberries, sugar, water, cornstarch, lemon juice, and vanilla. Stir continuously until the mixture thickens and the blueberries begin to break down, about 10 minutes. Remove from heat and let cool slightly.

7. Once the cake has cooled, with the end of a wooden spoon or wooden dowel, poke roughly 75 holes throughout the cake. Pour the blueberry sauce over the cake, making sure the berries and sauce sink into the holes. Set aside.

8. Prepare the cream cheese frosting. In a medium bowl with an electric hand mixer, cream the cream cheese, powdered sugar, and vanilla until light and fluffy.

9. In a separate medium bowl with an electric hand mixer, whip the heavy cream until stiff peaks form. Fold the whipped cream into the cream cheese mixture until evenly combined.

10. Dollop the cream cheese frosting over the blueberry layer and spread evenly. Refrigerate the cake for at least 1 hour, best overnight, before serving. Garnish with fresh blueberries before serving.

NSFW POKE CAKE

FOR THE CAKE

2 cups (250 g) all-purpose flour

2 cups (400 g) granulated sugar

¾ cup (75 g) unsweetened cocoa powder

2 teaspoons baking powder

1½ teaspoons baking soda

1 teaspoon salt

1 cup (240 g) buttermilk

½ cup (120 g) vegetable oil

2 large eggs

2 teaspoons vanilla extract

½ cup (120 g) hot brewed coffee

FOR THE FILLING

Two 14-ounce cans sweetened condensed milk

¼ cup (57 g) unsalted butter

FOR THE TOPPING

2 cups (490 g) heavy whipping cream

Four 1.4-ounce toffee chocolate bars, crushed

I must have been about eight years old when I first tried this cake, famously known as Better Than Sex Cake. Try explaining that name to an eight-year-old! Back then, there weren't many filters in my household, so I just shrugged it off. But after tasting it, my young mind was genuinely worried that I would forever compare sex to this cake because, well, the cake was better, right? As I grew older, I realized the humor behind the name.

To safeguard future youth from my irrational fear, I've renamed it NSFW Poke Cake. Instead of using a boxed devil's food cake, I make a chocolate cake that incorporates hot coffee to enhance the chocolate flavor. I also caramelize one can of sweetened condensed milk to add a touch of caramel without overwhelming sweetness. For the topping, I use unsweetened whipped cream to balance out the sweetness of the cake.

1. Preheat your oven to 350° F and spray a 9-by-13-inch baking pan with baking spray. Set aside.
2. Prepare the cake. In a medium bowl, whisk together the flour, sugar, cocoa powder, baking powder, baking soda, and salt until evenly combined. Make a well in the center of the dry ingredients.
3. Add the buttermilk, vegetable oil, eggs, and vanilla extract to the center of the well and whisk together until evenly combined. Whisk in the hot coffee until the batter is smooth.
4. Pour the batter into the prepared pan and spread evenly. Bake for 30 to 40 minutes, or until a toothpick or cake tester inserted in the middle comes out clean. Place on a wire rack and let cool.

NSFW Poke Cake only gets better with time—the longer it sets in the fridge, the richer and more irresistible it becomes.

5 Meanwhile, prepare the filling. In a medium saucepan over medium-low heat, add 1 can of the condensed milk and stir constantly until reduced and the color has darkened, 10 to 15 minutes. Lower the heat and add the remaining condensed milk and butter and whisk vigorously until the butter melts and the mixture is evenly combined. Set aside.

6 Once the cake has cooled, with the end of a wooden spoon or wooden dowel, poke roughly 75 holes throughout the cake. Pour the caramelized condensed milk over the cake making sure it sinks into the holes.

7 Make the topping. In a medium bowl with an electric hand mixer, whip the heavy cream until stiff peaks form, 1 to 2 minutes. Spread evenly over the cake. Scatter the toffee candy over the whipped cream. Chill in the refrigerator for at least 1 hour, best overnight, before serving.

SAUCEPAN BROWNIES

1¼ cups (270 g) granulated sugar
½ cup (120 g) dark brown sugar
2 teaspoons vanilla extract
4 eggs
1½ cups (195 g) cake flour
1 teaspoon kosher salt
½ cup (88 g) milk chocolate chips
1 cup (227 g) unsalted butter
¼ cup (52 g) vegetable oil
⅔ cup (65 g) unsweetened cocoa powder
2 teaspoons instant coffee
One 12-ounce bag semi-sweet chocolate chips

Nothing is more quintessential to a potluck than a pan of chewy, fudgy, rich chocolate brownies. Achieving that coveted cracked top? It's all in the technique: whisking eggs and sugar until airy, then slowly incorporating a hot chocolate mixture, whisking vigorously to create a glossy, chocolatey base before gently folding in the dry ingredients. For an extra boost of chocolatey goodness, I bloom cocoa powder in a mix of melted butter and oil, then melt in semi-sweet chocolate chips. This recipe moves quickly, so it's wise to have all your ingredients prepped before starting to minimize stress. Pop the brownies in the fridge for an hour after baking to lock in that irresistibly chewy texture. The anticipation is real, but trust me—the wait is well worth it.

1 Preheat your oven to 350° F and spray a 9-by-9-inch (or 8-by-8-inch) pan with baking spray, then line with parchment paper, leaving an overhang on two sides of the pan. Spray the parchment paper with baking spray and set aside.

2 In a medium bowl, add the granulated sugar, dark brown sugar, and vanilla. Whisk together to combine. Add the eggs and whisk vigorously until fully incorporated and the mixture is light yellow and frothy. Set aside.

3 In a separate medium bowl, add the cake flour, salt, and milk chocolate chips. Whisk together to combine. Set aside.

4 In a medium saucepan, add the butter and oil and melt over medium heat. Once melted, add the cocoa powder and instant coffee, whisking vigorously until smooth with no visible clumps.

continues

5 Reduce the heat to low and add the semi-sweet chocolate, stirring to melt with a wooden spoon. If the chocolate mixture starts to boil, remove the pan from the heat and continue stirring. Return the pan to the heat to continue melting the chocolate chips until smooth and glossy.

6 Moving quickly, slowly pour the hot chocolate mixture into the sugar-egg mixture while whisking continuously. You are tempering the eggs; pouring the hot mixture in too quickly will cook the eggs. Once all the hot mixture is poured, begin whisking vigorously to incorporate and fully dissolve most of the sugar—a few grains of sugar are fine; you don't want a very coarse mixture.

7 Add the flour mixture into the chocolate-egg mixture and, with a wooden spoon, fold in the dry ingredients to combine until no visible flour streaks remain—do not overmix.

8 Pour the batter into the prepared pan, smooth it evenly, and give the pan a few taps to release any air bubbles. Bake until the top is dry and slightly cracked, and a toothpick inserted in the middle comes out with a few crumbs. Edges should look firm and the center moist but not gooey, 25 to 30 minutes.

9 Remove from the oven and immediately place in the refrigerator to chill for 1 hour. Once cooled, remove the brownies by pulling them up from the overhang. Cut the brownies into servings.

Note: Placing the hot brownies in the refrigerator is optional, but the process does yield a more chewy, melt-in-your mouth brownie.

HEIRLOOM RECIPES

I REMEMBER the day I left for Boston; a decision made on a whim that would reshape the course of my life. Emotions ran high, unspoken words hung in the air, but it was a necessary step. In that bittersweet farewell, my grandmother handed me a weathered scrapbook, a culinary treasure trove of my favorite family recipes.

The pages within that leather-bound relic contained more than just ingredients and instructions. They were fragments of my childhood, snippets of love and care woven into each dish. Those recipes, including some from magazines and food packages, carefully curated from generations before me, became the textbook of my culinary roots. As I left on my journey, that scrapbook became a lifeline to my roots with its fragile pages and snapshots of nostalgia.

But that initial gift was just the beginning. Years later, after my grandmother's passing, I inherited more scrapbooks, each a testament to the culinary legacy of my family. Despite the complexities of our relationships and a less-than-glamorous history, food remained the common thread binding us together. As the guardian of these recipes, I am responsible for continuing their legacy, contributing my narrative as I share them with my son, Jasper, husband, Louis, and chosen families.

Heirloom recipes are more than just culinary artifacts. They are the stories passed down through generations, often either named after their creators or dedi-

AND ORAL HISTORY

cated to family members. These recipes fill the gaps in family history, connecting the dots when official records may be scarce. The kitchen is a vault for our pasts, where we unravel the threads of our identity.

This tradition extends beyond blood families. In the LGBTQIA+ community, where some face estrangement or lack of support, individuals leave their homes, taking with them the recipes that defined their childhoods. Enter chosen families and queer potlucks, where the exchange of recipes becomes a pivotal moment in rewriting our narratives.

Within the safe spaces of these gatherings, we share recipes and the oral history intertwined with them. Over time, heirloom recipes transform from symbols of grief and loss into emblems of growth and pride. It's a way for the LGBTQIA+ community to reshape perceptions, challenging gender norms in the kitchen and reclaiming food as a medium for storytelling.

As I write this cookbook, I realize it's not just a collection of recipes. It's my version of a scrapbook, a compilation of dishes that have accompanied me to self-acceptance. For those who find themselves alone or have chosen a different path, I implore you to hold on to the recipes that shaped your past. They are yours, a tangible connection to your story, a reminder of where you came from and where you're going.

GRASSHOPPER BROWNIES

FOR THE BROWNIES

1 cup (200 g) granulated sugar
½ cup (120 g) dark brown sugar
2 teaspoons vanilla extract
4 eggs
1¼ cups (156 g) all-purpose flour
1 teaspoon kosher salt
1 cup (227 g) unsalted butter
½ cup (52 g) vegetable oil
⅔ cup (65 g) unsweetened cocoa powder
2 teaspoons instant coffee
One 12-ounce bag semi-sweet chocolate chips

FOR THE FILLING

1 cup (227 g) unsalted butter, room temperature
2 cups (226 g) powdered sugar
3 tablespoons heavy whipping cream
½ teaspoon peppermint extract
2 or 3 drops green food coloring
½ cup (85 g) mini semi-sweet chocolate chips

FOR THE TOPPING

½ cup (113 g) unsalted butter
1 cup (175 g) dark chocolate chips

During summers as a kid, I couldn't get enough of Schwan's Silvermint bars (now Yelloh!)—those mint ice cream bars coated in rich chocolate were my ultimate treat. Even in high school, I'd jazz up boxed brownies with crushed mints on top for that extra minty kick. To this day, if Andes mints are offered after a meal at a restaurant, you can bet I'm grabbing a handful on the way out. Chocolate and mint speak to my soul.

These brownies are a variation of my Saucepan Brownies (page 29), but with a few changes: I've reduced the sugar to balance out the sweetness of the buttercream, and I've switched from cake flour to all-purpose flour to support the weight of the buttercream and ganache topping. The result? A decadent chocolate brownie with a sweet, minty topping complemented by a rich dark chocolate ganache and mini chocolate chips for added texture.

1 Preheat your oven to 350° F. Spray a 9-by-13-inch baking pan with baking spray, then line with parchment paper, leaving an overhang on two sides of the pan. Spray the parchment. Set aside.

2 Make the brownies. In a medium bowl, add the granulated sugar, dark brown sugar, and vanilla. Whisk together to combine. Add the eggs and whisk vigorously until fully incorporated and the mixture is light yellow and frothy. Set aside.

3 In a separate medium bowl, add the flour and salt and whisk together to combine. Set aside.

4 In a medium saucepan, add the butter and oil and melt over medium heat. Once melted, add the cocoa powder and instant coffee, whisking vigorously until smooth with no visible clumps.

5. Reduce the heat to low and add the semi-sweet chocolate chips, stirring to melt with a wooden spoon. If the chocolate mixture starts to boil, remove the pan from the heat and continue stirring until smooth and glossy.

6. Moving quickly, slowly pour the hot chocolate mixture into the sugar-egg mixture while whisking continuously. You are tempering the eggs; pouring the hot mixture in too quickly will cook the eggs. Once all the hot mixture is poured, begin whisking vigorously to incorporate and fully dissolve most of the sugar—a few grains of sugar are fine.

7. Add the flour mixture into the chocolate-egg mixture and, with a wooden spoon, fold in the dry ingredients to combine until no visible flour streaks remain—do not overmix.

8. Pour the batter into the prepared pan, smooth it evenly, and give the pan a few taps to release any air bubbles. Bake until the top is dry and slightly cracked, and a toothpick inserted in the middle comes out with a few crumbs. Edges should look firm and the center moist but not gooey, 25 to 30 minutes.

9. Remove from the oven and immediately place in the refrigerator to chill for 1 hour.

10. Meanwhile, prepare the filling . In a medium bowl with an electric hand mixer, cream together the butter and powdered sugar until light and fluffy, 2 to 3 minutes. Stop the mixer and add the heavy cream and peppermint extract. Mix on medium until evenly combined and the mixture is fluffy, 1 to 2 minutes. Add the green food coloring and mix until evenly blended and pale green. With a rubber spatula, fold in the mini chocolate chips until evenly combined.

11. Remove the brownies from the refrigerator and evenly spread the buttercream over the brownies and return to the refrigerator for 30 minutes for the buttercream to firm up.

12. Meanwhile, prepare the chocolate topping. In a small heatproof bowl, add the butter and dark chocolate chips. Using a microwave, melt in 30-second intervals, stopping and stirring, until the butter and chocolate are melted. Whisk together to evenly combine.

13 Remove the brownies from the refrigerator and pour the chocolate over the buttercream layer. With an offset spatula or the back of a spoon, spread into an even layer. Return to the refrigerator and chill for another 30 minutes.

14 Once the chocolate is set, remove the brownies by pulling them up from the overhang. Cut the brownies into servings.

BAKING TIP: GETTING THE MOST FLAVOR OUT OF YOUR COCOA POWDER

The technique of blooming cocoa powder is a little baking secret that can seriously up your chocolate game. It's a trick pastry chefs swear by for getting intense flavors and perfect textures.

So, what's the deal with blooming? Cocoa powder is made from dehydrated cocoa solids ground into powder. However, a thin membrane can stick to these cocoa solids during processing, hiding between the bean and its shell. Blooming helps break down this membrane, exposing more cocoa solids and increasing the flavor. It can also improve the texture of your baked goods, giving them a smoother, more velvety finish. It's perfect for cakes, brownies, and any chocolatey treats.

To bloom your cocoa powder, pop it into a heatproof bowl and add a hot liquid like water, coffee, melted butter, or oil (warmed not boiling)—whatever liquid the recipe calls for. Stir until smooth, then let it cool while you prep everything else. Cooling is crucial here unless the recipe calls for adding hot liquid.

A quick tip: Don't let your cocoa powder bloom too long, or it might turn bitter. This isn't an all-night process—just a few minutes will do. And don't worry; whether you're using natural or Dutch-processed cocoa powder, you can still give it a bloom. So go ahead and give your cocoa powder a little extra love!

FINDING CO
IN THE TOUGH

WHEN I WAS between the ages of 18 and 19, I went on an eight-month adventure living on a bus, traveling throughout the United States, the United Kingdom, and Spain with the Continental Singers, a Christian performing arts group. This came after four eye-opening months in Orange County, where a chance encounter at a grocery store sent me backward. A guy came up to me, asked me out, and gave me his number. It was a big deal for me—my first time being asked out by a guy, my first nonverbal acknowledgment of being gay, and my first taste of mutual attraction. But despite the unwavering support of my queer chosen family, I wasn't yet ready to fully embrace my gay identity back then.

Feeling conflicted, I joined The Continental Singers, influenced by my strong, conflicting, religious beliefs. I believed if I went on tour and surrounded myself with fellow Christians, I could reset myself and get back on "the right track." The tour's strict rules, such as no secular music, alcohol, smoking, certain attire, mingling with the opposite sex, relationships, or any hint of homosexuality, posed a challenge. Despite grappling with these rules and the organization's doctrine internally, I found comfort in the company of like-minded people, especially my close friend who I'll call Tim.

Tim and I became inseparable, forming a strong bond that helped us navigate our paths of self-discovery. We had to keep our friendship discreet, understanding that our connection was more than just friendship, even though we never explicitly labeled it. We kept our truth hidden, presenting ourselves as "just friends."

The LGBTQIA+ community has an incredible ability to find acceptance and

MMUNITY
EST PLACES

friendship, even in tough situations. This was evident in secret queer potlucks, where a group of lesbians in San Francisco started clandestine gatherings around food, creating a safe space for queer people to connect. Tim and I did something similar; among about 30 teenagers and young adults, we quietly found kindred spirits within the conservative group. Our group included people with diverse beliefs—some religious but challenging the strict rules, others identifying as bisexual or lesbian, and a few outwardly religious but agnostic or atheist at heart, touring just to please their families. There were about 10 of us, and we became each other's chosen family on tour. We fit in with the larger group, staying close while at our host homes or discreetly separating during outings to find comfort away from the more religious members.

During our travels, we rarely stayed in hotels, often staying with host families from the churches where we performed. Despite my changing beliefs, I cherished the hospitality of church members, who welcomed us into their homes and shared their lives. We had many church potluck meals during our travels, with each host family bringing a dish before performances. For eight months, I ate from rectangular pans and foil tins. During that time, external uniformity was required, with the layers of texture and depth hidden from view, representing necessary boundaries in my life. Looking back, I see the resilience of the LGBTQIA+ community and our ability to find acceptance and support, even in challenging environments. We shared meals, stories, and experiences, forming bonds that helped us navigate life together.

NSFW Poke Cake (page 27)

Grasshopper Brownies (page 35)

Cheers to Butter Pecan Icebox Cake (page 160)!

Is it breakfast, lunch, or the perfect dinner side? It's Gooey Butter Corn Cake (page 116)—a delicious mystery!

HUMMINGBIRD BLONDIES

FOR THE CREAM CHEESE SWIRL

- One 8-ounce block cream cheese, room temperature
- ¼ cup (28 g) powdered sugar
- 1 egg
- ½ teaspoon vanilla extract

FOR THE BLONDIES

- ¼ cup (50 g) granulated sugar
- 2 teaspoons vanilla extract
- 3 eggs
- 1¾ cups (218 g) all-purpose flour
- 1 teaspoon kosher salt
- 2 teaspoons ground cinnamon
- 1 cup (120 g) pecans, chopped
- 1 banana, very ripe
- One 8-ounce can crushed pineapple, juices drained
- 1 cup (227 g) unsalted butter
- 1½ cups (330 g) light brown sugar

Touring with a faith-based performing arts group while in my late teens was an adventure that didn't put me back on the straight and narrow as planned. Still, it did introduce me to some incredible food during our cross-country travels. One culinary gem I discovered was the hummingbird cake, a Southern "staple" brought to the States from Jamaica in the 1960s. It consists of layers of spiced cake filled with bananas and pineapples topped with cream cheese frosting—carrot cake's cousin. It was a potluck favorite, but its tall, uncut slices and tendency to tilt in warm weather made it less than ideal for sharing.

To solve this, I created hummingbird blondies—a portable, potluck-friendly version of the classic cake. Making these blondies are a bit of a labor of love and require tempering eggs, but trust me the process is easy to execute. Just take your time. The outcome produces blondies that are moist and chewy, with a cream cheese layer to balance the fruity sweetness. After baking, chilling them in the fridge for an hour locks in moisture and gives them a dense, chewy texture. The aroma as they bake is irresistible, and when you take your first bite, you'll already start anticipating your next helping. Sorry, not sorry.

1. Preheat your oven to 350° F and spray a 9-by-9-inch (or 8-by-8-inch) pan with baking spray, then line with parchment paper, leaving an overhang on two sides of the pan. Spray the parchment paper with baking spray and set aside.
2. For the cream cheese swirl, combine the cream cheese, powdered sugar, egg, and vanilla extract in a small bowl. Using an electric hand mixer with beater attachments on medium speed, blend until smooth for 2 to 3 minutes. Set aside.

continues →

3. For the blondies, whisk together by hand the granulated sugar and vanilla in a medium bowl. Add the eggs and whisk vigorously until thoroughly combined and the mixture becomes slightly frothy and light yellow. Set aside.
4. In a separate medium bowl, whisk together by hand the flour, salt, cinnamon, and pecans. Set aside.
5. With a fork, mash the banana in a separate small bowl until mostly smooth, leaving a few clumps. Add the drained crushed pineapple to the mashed banana. Set aside.
6. In a medium saucepan over medium heat, melt the butter and light brown sugar, stirring occasionally with a wooden spoon until the sugar dissolves and the mixture is smooth and bubbling around the edges. Remove from the heat.
7. Moving quickly, slowly pour the hot sugar mixture, a ¼ cup at a time, into the sugar-egg mixture while whisking by hand continuously to temper the eggs. Whisk vigorously until most of the sugar is dissolved. Whisk in the banana and pineapple until combined.
8. Add the flour mixture to the sugar-egg mixture and fold in with a wooden spoon until no visible flour streaks remain—do not overmix.
9. Pour the batter into the prepared pan, smooth it evenly, and tap the pan to release any air bubbles.
10. With a spoon, dollop the cream cheese mixture on top of the batter randomly, then swirl it into the batter with a butter knife until evenly spread.
11. Bake for 30 to 35 minutes until golden brown, the edges are slightly pulled away from the pan, and the cream cheese is puffed up. Insert a toothpick in the center, which should come out with a few crumbs.
12. Remove from the oven and immediately place in the refrigerator to chill for at least 1 hour, preferably overnight, for best results. Once cooled, lift the blondies out of the pan using the parchment paper overhang. Cut into servings.

BLUEBERRY-AMARETTO BARS

- 1¾ cups (210 g) graham cracker crumbs
- ½ cup (113 g) unsalted butter, melted
- ¾ cup (150 g) granulated sugar
- 2 large eggs
- One 8-ounce package cream cheese, softened
- Two 3.4-ounce packages instant vanilla pudding
- 2½ cups (600 g) whole milk
- ½ cup (120 g) amaretto, divided
- 1¼ cups (160 g) cornstarch
- 5 cups (750 g) blueberries
- 1 cup (240 g) heavy cream
- ¼ cup (28 g) powdered sugar
- 1 teaspoon vanilla extract

I once crossed paths with a fiery old lady at a church potluck. She had this eccentric vibe, and I swear she must've been a Woodstock-goer back in the day. I was 18, and she strolled up to me and my friends with a platter of blueberry squares. She'd been eyeing us all day, so it wasn't a total shock when she finally made her move. Passing us the squares, she leaned in and whispered, "Don't share these with the other churchgoers; these are only for our kind of people. Our community is everywhere!" We took a bite, and to my surprise, the blueberry squares were spiked with amaretto. She was right; our people are everywhere!

1. Preheat your oven to 350° F and spray a 9-by-13-inch pan with baking spray. Set aside.
2. In a medium bowl, combine the graham cracker crumbs, melted butter, and ¼ cup (50 g) of the granulated sugar. Press the mixture into the bottom of the prepared pan.
3. In another medium bowl, beat the eggs, ¼ cup (50 g) sugar, and cream cheese with an electric hand mixer until smooth. Pour the mixture over the crust and bake for 25 to 30 minutes, or until set and slightly jiggly in the middle. Cool completely on a wire rack.
4. In a separate medium bowl, whisk together the pudding mix, whole milk, and ¼ cup (60 ml) of the amaretto until smooth. Pour the pudding over the cooled cream cheese layer. Chill in the refrigerator for at least 30 minutes.

5. In a medium saucepan over medium heat, combine the cornstarch and remaining ¼ cup sugar. Gradually add the remaining ¼ cup amaretto, stirring until smooth. Add the blueberries and cook, stirring occasionally, until thickened. Remove from heat and let cool completely.
6. Pour the blueberry mixture over the pudding layer. Cover with plastic wrap and chill in the refrigerator for at least 4 hours or overnight.
7. Before serving, make the whipped cream: In a medium bowl, whip the heavy cream, powdered sugar, and vanilla extract with an electric hand mixer until stiff peaks form. Spread over the chilled dessert. Cut into squares and serve.

CHERRY-ALMOND PIE BARS

FOR THE BARS

1 cup (227 g) unsalted butter, softened

½ cup (100 g) granulated sugar

2 cups (250 g) all-purpose flour

¼ teaspoon kosher salt

Two 21-ounce cans cherry pie filling

FOR THE CRUMBLE TOPPING

½ cup (113 g) unsalted butter, melted

1 cup (200 g) granulated sugar

1 cup (125 g) all-purpose flour

¼ cup (20 g) sliced almonds

Pinch of kosher salt

FOR THE ALMOND DRIZZLE

½ cup (56 g) powdered sugar

¼ cup (60 g) heavy whipping cream

¼ teaspoon almond extract

When I get the chance to add a burst of color to my baking, I'm all over it. These bars are a prime example, with their vivid ruby-red cherries peeking out from under the crumbly topping. I go easy on the crumble, letting it add just a hint of depth so the cherries can steal the spotlight. The salty shortbread crust provides a nice contrast to the tart cherries and sweet, almond-scented crumble. It's all about letting those colors shine!

1. Preheat your oven to 350° F and spray a 9-by-13-inch sheet pan with baking spray. Set aside.
2. Make the bars. In a medium bowl with an electric hand mixer, cream together the butter and sugar until light and fluffy. Add the flour and salt, and mix until crumbly.
3. Press the mixture into the bottom of the prepared pan to form an even layer. Bake the crust for 15 to 20 minutes until lightly golden brown. Remove from the oven.
4. Spread the cherry pie filling over the partially baked crust.
5. Make the crumble topping. In a medium bowl, combine the butter, sugar, flour, sliced almonds, and salt. With a fork, mix until crumbly.
6. Sprinkle the crumble topping evenly over the cherry pie filling. Bake for an additional 25 to 30 minutes, or until golden brown and the cherry filling bubbles.
7. Cool on a wire rack until completely cool .
8. Meanwhile, make the almond drizzle. In a small bowl, whisk together the powdered sugar, heavy whipping cream, and almond extract until smooth.
9. Once the bars are cooled, using a whisk or spoon, top the bars with the almond drizzle.

A YEARLY VISITOR, A MANDARIN ORANGE CAKE, AND A LESSON IN LIVING AUTHENTICALLY

BACK IN the day, my grandma's good friend Shirley was a yearly visitor; boy, she was a force to be reckoned with. Shirley, a wild spirit from Oregon, cruising down on her Harley, radiating free-spirited vibes, tenacity, and a level of self-confidence that screamed, "I know who I am, and I love myself!" When word got out that Shirley was coming, it meant a couple of things to me.

Firstly, it meant quality time with my buddy, who would entertain me for hours with stories of her adventures and sprinkle in little nuggets of wisdom on living authentically. My gut feeling? Shirley probably knew me better than I knew myself and used our time together to equip me with the skills to navigate life on my terms.

The other exciting aspect of Shirley's visit? The guarantee of her infamous cake—we called it Shirley's Cake. It was a straightforward yet grand creation with three layers and dollops of sweet but not overly sweet pineapple frosting. This kickass cake, made by a kickass woman who rode Harleys, became a family treasure. For me, it holds even more significance as it was the dessert I brought to my first queer potluck.

Perhaps subconsciously, I was channeling Shirley's grit and zest for life, or maybe it was just a knee-jerk reaction. This cake was our family's go-to, our default when faced with culinary indecision and anxiety. Regardless, this cake symbolizes the inception of me embracing the life lessons Shirley planted all those years ago.

SHIRLEY'S CAKE

One 16½-ounce yellow cake mix (classic yellow or butter recipe)

4 eggs

One 15-ounce can mandarin oranges with juices, plus more for garnish, if desired

½ cup (100 g) vegetable oil

½ cup (113 g) unsalted butter, melted

One 8-ounce container whipped topping

One 3.4-ounce package instant vanilla pudding

Two 8-ounce cans crushed pineapple

Some of you might recognize this as the mandarin orange cake it is. It's a classic home recipe made with boxed yellow cake mix with a twist—discard the instructions and throw in a few additional ingredients. The frosting? Whipped topping jazzed up with instant vanilla pudding mix and crushed pineapple.

Admittedly, this is the only recipe in the book that I didn't completely make my own. I had to decipher my grandmother's vague recipe descriptions, adjusting quantities based on instinct. I even threw in ½ cup of melted unsalted butter to elevate the cake's flavor—oil for moisture, butter for richness.

I adore the cake in three layers, but it's only appropriate for a potluck to make it in a single layer using a 9-by-13-inch pan. Feel like doing a bit extra? Score the cake into portions and crown the center of each square with a mandarin orange slice. It's a nod to Shirley's legacy—a kickass cake for a kickass life.

1. Preheat your oven to 350°F and spray a 9-by-13-inch pan with baking spray and set aside.

2. In a medium bowl, blend together cake mix, eggs, mandarin oranges, oil, and butter with a hand mixer with the beater attachments on medium-high speed until fully incorporated and the mandarin oranges have broken down into little pieces—2 to 3 minutes.

3. Pour the batter into the prepared pan and evenly spread, giving the pan a few taps on the counter to remove any air bubbles. Bake for 30 minutes, or until golden brown and a toothpick inserted in the middle of the cake comes out clean. Remove from the oven and cool completely on a wire rack.

continues

4 While the cake cools, make the topping. In a separate medium bowl, blend together the whipped topping, vanilla pudding, and crushed pineapple with a hand mixer with the beater attachment on medium speed until fully incorporated.

5 Once the cake is completely cooled, pour the topping over the cake and smooth evenly with the back of a wooden spoon or offset spatula. Cover with plastic wrap and chill in the refrigerator overnight.

6 When ready to serve, score and portion the cake, and if desired, top with a mandarin orange slice and mint leaf in the center of each portion.

BOXED MIXES ARE INGREDIENTS

IT HAS ALWAYS puzzled me why we treat boxed mixes like they're the villains of the culinary world—especially in baking. Boxed cake mixes, pudding mixes, and their kin are there for a reason—or several reasons. As kids, these pantry staples were our parents' go-to for quick, delicious treats. We didn't question it; we just knew it worked like a charm.

But then I grew up and ventured into the world of professional baking and food writing. With it came this unspoken rule that boxed mixes were inferior to from-scratch recipes. I wanted to fit in, so I tossed aside these humble ingredients like a guilty secret. I ignored that they were my starting point as a self-taught baker, and I was too embarrassed to admit it. As a food writer, I bought into the idea that everything had to be made from scratch, regardless of time constraints or limited access to alternative ingredients. But it didn't sit right with me.

Why do we feel the need to classify ingredients and send out these subtle messages that your pantry and kitchen time determine your worth, class, and acceptance? It's a bizarre form of culinary classism that I couldn't get behind.

Boxed mixes are ingredients with a purpose at home and in a professional kitchen. They're not lazy or low brow; it's all about perspective. They're like the queer folks at a potluck—often underestimated but bringing their unique flavor to the table.

Just as we shouldn't label or place expectations on people, the same goes for ingredients. Let's break free from the chains of culinary classism and embrace the convenience, versatility, and, yes, the sheer magic that boxed mixes bring to our kitchens.

They're not shortcuts; intentionally reaching for them is a choice to create something delicious and shareable. Recipes vary in time, ingredients, and process—one isn't better than the other. The same goes for people who love and identify differently than society dictates.

There is nothing wrong, embarrassing, or lazy about using boxed mixes. They provide a foundation for creativity or serve as an ingredient with straightforward directions for making something delicious and comforting. And if you find yourself grabbing that boxed cake mix and premade frosting because you want cake right now. Go for it; eat the boxed cake and be queer!

YOU'RE NOT LAZY, DAISY CAKE

FOR THE CAKE

- 1 cup (125 g) all-purpose flour
- 1 cup (120 g) cake flour
- 2½ teaspoons baking powder
- 1 teaspoon kosher salt
- ½ teaspoon ground cinnamon
- ¼ teaspoon ground nutmeg
- ¼ teaspoon ground clove
- 4 eggs
- 2 cups (400 g) granulated sugar
- 1 teaspoon vanilla extract
- 1 cup (240 g) whole milk
- ¾ cup (170 g) unsalted butter

FOR THE COCONUT TOPPING

- ¾ cup (170 g) unsalted butter
- 1¼ cups (275 g) light brown sugar
- ½ cup (120 g) heavy whipping cream
- Pinch of kosher salt
- 2 cups (160 g) sweetened shredded coconut

This cake is actually called Lazy Daisy Cake, but I take issue with names suggesting any recipe is "lazy." It's an old-fashioned cake recipe that probably got the name for not having to frost the cake. Instead, the topping is poured over the almost-finished cake and put back in the oven to finish. Regardless of how long it takes you to make it, you're putting in the effort. We shouldn't categorize the quality of desserts based on the difficulty level of the execution. That's nonsense. So here's my version, and it's fantastic.

I don't have a backstory to this recipe, but I did find it in a stack of old family recipes. I like to imagine that my great-great-grandmother Daisy made this. Most Daisy cakes are made with a yellow cake, but this version is from someone in my family who used a spiced cake, which is an excellent complement to the sweet coconut topping that gets broiled in the last few minutes of baking. The result is a deliciously caramelized, crispy edged, and super moist cake. Whoever came up with this recipe was by no means lazy—that's some genius baking!

1. Preheat your oven to 350° F and butter a 9-by-13-inch pan. Set aside.
2. Make the cake: In a medium bowl, whisk together the flours, baking powder, salt, cinnamon, nutmeg, and clove until combined.
3. In a separate medium bowl, whisk together the eggs, sugar, and vanilla extract. Add the dry ingredients to the wet ingredients and whisk together until evenly combined.

continues

4 In a small saucepan over medium heat, add the milk and butter. Stirring occasionally, bring to just a boil, making sure the butter is melted.

5 Slowly pour the hot butter-milk mixture into the batter, whisking continuously until the batter is smooth and evenly combined. Pour the batter into the prepared pan and bake for 20 to 25 minutes, or until just about done (a slight jiggle in the center).

6 Meanwhile, prepare the coconut topping. In a medium saucepan over medium heat, melt the butter. Once melted add the brown sugar, heavy whipping cream, and salt. Stir until combined and the sugar is dissolved, but not boiling. Remove from heat and fold in the coconut.

7 Remove the cake from the oven and turn your oven to broil. Carefully pour the coconut topping over the cake and spread in an even layer. Broil for 4 to 5 minutes, or until the topping is bubbling and the coconut is toasted. Carefully rotate the cake periodically to ensure an even caramelization. Cool completely on a wire rack before serving.

Note: Keep the oven door slightly cracked open when broiling the top of the cake, watching carefully to make sure the cake doesn't burn.

WACKY CAKE

FOR THE CAKE

- ½ cup (120 g) freshly brewed coffee
- ¼ cup plus 1 tablespoon (32 g) unsweetened cocoa powder
- 2¼ cups (280 g) all-purpose flour
- 1½ cups (300 g) granulated sugar
- 2 teaspoons baking soda
- 1 teaspoon kosher salt
- ⅔ cup (147 g) vegetable oil
- 4½ teaspoons white vinegar
- 1½ teaspoons vanilla extract
- 1 cup (240 g) cold water

FOR THE FROSTING

- One 8-ounce package cream cheese, room temperature
- 2 cups (226 g) powdered sugar
- ¼ cup (62 g) heavy whipping cream

This cake—from my hometown—was legendary, and it had somewhat of a cult following. Every Thursday in elementary school, the cafeteria served chili cheese nachos and wacky cake for lunch: A square slice of chocolate cake topped with mysterious white frosting (I think it was old-fashioned frosting). These days, this cake isn't just for elementary school lunches: It is now a staple at gatherings in my hometown, from weddings to baby showers to birthdays. It's so popular that it earned a dedicated Facebook page, with various recipes posted vying for the original title. But what exactly is wacky cake? It's a Depression-era dessert made without dairy or eggs that relies on vinegar and baking soda for leavening. Plus you mix the ingredients right in the pan! In my version, I reduce the amount of cold water and add hot coffee to enhance the chocolate flavor. Also I bloom the cocoa powder and use a cream cheese frosting to replicate the mysterious, shiny, smooth frosting. I keep the practice of mixing all the ingredients in the baking pan because it's fun. For the best taste, serve it chilled. Welcome to the cult!

1. Preheat your oven to 350° F.
2. Make the cake. In a small bowl, whisk together the coffee and cocoa powder until the cocoa powder is dissolved and smooth. Set aside.
3. In a 9-by-13-inch pan, add the flour, sugar, baking soda, and salt. Mix with a fork until combined.

Note: You do not need to grease the pan; the cake has enough oil, and it won't stick.

4 Make a well in the center of the flour mixture. Add the oil, vinegar, vanilla extract, coffee-cocoa mixture, and water. Mix vigorously, using the fork in a whisk motion, until well combined and no visible flour or oil remains.

5 Bake for 20 to 25 minutes, or until the top springs back when touched and a toothpick or cake tester inserted in the middle comes out clean. Remove the cake from the oven and cool on a wire rack until room temperature.

6 To make the frosting, add the cream cheese, powdered sugar, and heavy whipping cream to a medium bowl. With an electric hand mixer with the whisk attachment at medium-low speed, whisk together until smooth and shiny, with no visible clumps.

7 Once the cake is cooled, pour the frosting over it and smooth evenly using an offset spatula. Cover with plastic wrap and chill in the refrigerator for at least 1 hour before serving. The beauty of this cake is the frosting running down the sides and soaking into the cake.

Note: The frosting is very smooth and loose, don't expect a firm buttercream-like frosting.

STRAWBERRY AND CREAM CAKE

FOR THE CAKE

1 cup (150 g) strawberries, hulled

1 cup (200 g) granulated sugar

½ cup (100 g) vegetable oil

2 large eggs

1 teaspoon vanilla bean paste

2 cups (250 g) all-purpose flour

1 teaspoon baking powder

½ teaspoon baking soda

½ teaspoon kosher salt

1 cup (240 g) buttermilk

FOR THE TOPPING

1½ cups (360 g) heavy whipping cream

3 tablespoons powdered sugar

1 teaspoon vanilla bean paste

1 cup (150 g) shortbread cookies, crushed

1 cup (150 g) strawberries, hulled and chopped

I'm all for repurposing recipes and making a few tweaks to get a new creation. Take this cake, for example. It all started with my friend's nostalgia for those bright pink strawberry boxed cakes from childhood. When he wanted a fresh strawberry cake for his boyfriend's surprise 30th birthday, I eagerly volunteered.

After making that strawberry cake, it hit me: Why stop there? With a simple fruit swap and by reducing the puree to intensify its flavor, you can turn this strawberry and cream cake into a blueberry and cream cake, a peach and cream cake, or whatever fruit your heart desires. The same goes for the topping—use fresh fruit to match the puree in the cake. It's all about getting creative and making the recipe your own!

1. Preheat your oven to 350° F and spray a 9-by-13-inch pan with baking spray. Set aside.
2. Make the cake. Using a food processor, puree 1 cup strawberries. Pour in a medium saucepan over medium heat, stirring occasionally, and cook until the puree reduces by half. Set aside and let cool.
3. In a medium bowl, whisk together the sugar, vegetable oil, eggs, and vanilla bean paste.
4. In a separate medium bowl, sift together the flour, baking powder, baking soda, and salt.
5. Gradually add the dry ingredients to the wet ingredients, alternating with the buttermilk, until well combined. Fold in the cooled strawberry puree.

6 Pour the batter evenly into the prepared pan. Bake for 25 to 30 minutes, or until a toothpick or cake tester inserted into the center comes out clean. Cool completely on a wire rack.

7 Meanwhile, make the topping. In a medium bowl with an electric hand mixer, whip the heavy cream, powdered sugar, and vanilla bean paste until stiff peaks form.

8 Spread the whipped cream over the cooled cake. Sprinkle the crushed shortbread cookies over the whipped cream and top with chopped strawberries.

9 Chill in the refrigerator for at least 1 hour before serving.

CITRUS BAKEWELL

FOR THE CRUST

1⅔ cups (207 g) all-purpose flour

1 tablespoon powdered sugar

¼ teaspoon kosher salt

1 egg yolk

½ cup (113 g) unsalted butter, cold and cubed

2 to 3 tablespoons water, ice cold

FOR THE FRANGIPANE FILLING

¾ cup (150 g) granulated sugar

Zest of 1 orange

Zest of 1 lemon

1¼ cups (283 g) unsalted butter, room temperature

2 eggs

1 teaspoon vanilla extract

1½ cups (145 g) almond flour

1½ cups (470 g) marmalade

½ cup (47 g) sliced almonds

Powdered sugar for garnish

I spent a good chunk of time in the United Kingdom during my late teens and early 20s, taking a gap year (or two) before heading off to college. With my adventurous spirit and zero responsibilities, I jumped at the chance to live abroad. I highly recommend it to everyone—it's a fantastic way to reset your perspectives and experience new things outside your comfort zone.

Living in the UK exposed me to so much, but one thing that really stood out was the hospitality and genuine nature of it all. And, surprisingly, a lot of that warmth came in the form of a Bakewell cake. This traditional English dessert is a true delight, with its short-crust pastry shell filled with jam and almond-flavored frangipane (a sweet spreadable paste). I absolutely adored these treats, and whenever someone made one for me, I was over the moon. They're humble desserts baked with an immense amount of love.

You can use any jam you like, but I have a soft spot for the tangy kick that citrusy marmalade adds, which cuts through the sweetness of the frangipane. For me, a Bakewell is the perfect addition to any potluck—it's unexpected and brings a cozy bakery vibe that everyone can appreciate.

1 Prepare the crust. Using a food processor, pulse together the flour, powdered sugar, and salt until just combined. Add the egg yolk and pulse to combine.

2 Add the cubed cold butter and pulse until the mixture is coarse, like wet beach sand. Add the cold water a tablespoon at a time and pulse a few times until the mixture barely comes together. The dough will be crumbly.

continues

3 Lay out a piece of plastic wrap on the counter long enough to wrap the dough. Dump the dough in the center of the plastic wrap. Carefully pull each side of the plastic wrap, one side at a time over the dough, making a straight clean edge (you're trying to form the dough into a square). Once covered, gently press down on the dough with your hands to compress the dough together. Use your hands to mold the sides of the dough into a square. Chill in the refrigerator for at least 1 hour or overnight.

4 Preheat your oven to 350 °F and spray a 9-by-9-inch (or 8-by-8-inch) pan with baking spray and line with parchment paper both ways so all four sides have an overhang. Set aside.

Note: This helps remove the Bakewell from the pan and makes it easier to cut into portions, as the bake is delicate from the frangipane and marmalade.

5 Remove the dough from the refrigerator and dust a clean surface with flour. With a floured rolling pin, gently roll out the dough to ¼ inch thick. Don't worry if the dough cracks; you can use leftover dough to fill in the cracks. Cut a 10-by-10-inch square from the dough and carefully place in the prepared pan, folding the overhang up the side of the pan, making a little border around the edges. Prick the dough with a fork in several areas (this prevents the dough from rising too much) and blind bake for 10 to 15 minutes, or until the dough is lightly golden brown.

6 Meanwhile, prepare the frangipane filling. In a medium bowl, add the sugar, orange zest, and lemon zest. With your fingers, rub the zests and sugar together until combined to release the zests' natural oils. The sugar will turn slightly orange. Add the butter, and with an electric hand mixer, cream together until light and fluffy, 2 to 3 minutes.

7 Stop the mixer and add the eggs and vanilla. Mix until combined, about 1 minute. With a rubber spatula, fold in the almond flour until evenly combined. Set aside.

8 Once the crust has blind baked, remove from the oven and spread the marmalade evenly over the bottom. Top the marmalade layer with the frangipane, spreading in an even layer. Bake for 30 minutes.

9 Remove from the oven and sprinkle almonds over the top; return to the oven and bake for another 10 minutes or until the top is golden brown and visibly dry. Cool completely on a wire rack.

10 Before serving, remove the Bakewell from the pan using the parchment overhangs and portion. Dust with powdered sugar.

BAKING TIP: MAKE IT ZESTY

Adding zest is a fantastic way to boost the flavor of your baked goods and add a hint of acidity to balance out all the sweetness. But here's a quick trick to take your zesty flavor to the next level: Rub the zest and sugar together between your fingers before adding other ingredients into the mix. This releases the natural oils from the zest, perfuming the sugar and intensifying the citrus flavor.

This simple step enhances the flavor and ensures that the zest is distributed evenly throughout your bake because it prevents any clumps of zest. Plus, it tenderizes the zest, giving your baked goods a smoother texture. It's a small trick that delivers significant flavor benefits!

PEANUT BUTTER AND ROASTED RED GRAPE CHEESECAKE SQUARES

FOR THE GRAPES

1½ pounds seedless red grapes

2 tablespoons honey

FOR THE CRUST

1½ cups (180 g) graham cracker crumbs

¼ cup (50 g) granulated sugar

½ teaspoon kosher salt

½ cup (113 g) unsalted butter

FOR THE FILLING

Two 8 ounce packages cream cheese, room temperature

1 cup (260 g) creamy peanut butter

1 cup (200 g) granulated sugar

3 eggs

1 teaspoon vanilla extract

½ cup (120 g) half-and-half

FOR THE TOPPING

1 cup (240 g) sour cream

¼ cup (50 g) granulated sugar

1 teaspoon vanilla extract

These cheesecake bars genuinely capture the soul of a peanut butter and jelly sandwich. The cheesecake itself is peanut butter–based, and instead of swirling in grape jelly, I roast red seedless grapes tossed in honey. As they roast, the grapes intensify in flavor and naturally become jammy.

To top it off, a classic sour cream topping adds a thin, delicate layer that provides a bit of tang to balance out the peanut butter's richness and the grapes' sweetness. Just trust me on this one—these bars are a delightful twist on a classic combo.

1 Preheat your oven to 350°F. Line a sheet pan with parchment paper.

2 In a medium bowl, toss the grapes with honey. Evenly scatter the grapes on the prepared sheet pan and roast for 1 hour, occasionally stirring to roast evenly, until the grapes are wilted and juices release. Remove and cool on a wire rack.

Note: Grapes can be roasted a day before and stored in an airtight container in the refrigerator until ready to use.

3. To make the crust, leave the oven on and spray a 9-by-9-inch (or 8-by-8-inch) pan with baking spray and line it with parchment paper. Set aside. Fill a heatproof casserole dish or pan two-thirds full with water and place it in the center of the bottom rack of the oven.

Note: This method creates steam in the oven, which helps prevent the cheesecake from cracking, produces an even bake, and helps create a creamy center.

4. In a small bowl, whisk together the graham cracker crumbs, sugar, and salt. Add the butter and mix it with a fork until the mixture looks like wet beach sand, using the fork to break up any large clumps.

5. Pour the mixture into the prepared pan and press it into an even layer. Bake for 10 minutes; the crust will darken. Remove and cool completely on a wire rack.

6. Meanwhile, make the cheesecake filling. In a food processor, add the cream cheese, peanut butter, sugar, eggs, vanilla extract, and half-and-half. Pulse until fully incorporated and smooth, stopping a few times and scraping down the sides and bottom with a rubber spatula. Pour half the mixture over the cooled crust and smooth it into an even layer. Evenly scatter the grapes over the layer and top with the remaining cheesecake filling.

7. Bake for 50 to 60 minutes, or until the edges are set and the center slightly jiggles, like gelatin.

8. Meanwhile, make the sour cream topping. In a small bowl, whisk together the sour cream, sugar, and vanilla until evenly combined. Once the cheesecake is set, remove the pan from the oven and carefully pour the topping evenly over the cheesecake. Bake for another 15 to 20 minutes, or until the topping is set and glossy.

9. Turn off the oven, crack open the oven door slightly, and let the cheesecake cool inside the oven. It will be puffed up and slowly deflate as it cools. Let it cool in the warm oven, preventing it from cracking.

10. Once cooled, cover the pan with foil and refrigerate for at least 2 hours; it is best to cool overnight. Portion into squares and serve.

MAPLE-WALNUT CHEESECAKE SQUARES

FOR THE CRUST

1½ cups (180 g) graham cracker crumbs

2 tablespoons granulated sugar

¼ teaspoon kosher salt

½ cup (113 g) unsalted butter, melted

FOR THE FILLING

Two 8-ounce packages cream cheese, room temperature

¼ cup (50 g) granulated sugar

⅓ cup (100 g) real maple syrup

2 eggs

1 teaspoon vanilla extract

½ teaspoon maple extract

¼ cup (60 g) half-and-half

FOR THE TOPPING

1 cup (112 g) walnuts

⅓ cup (100 g) real maple syrup

2 tablespoons dark brown sugar

1 tablespoon unsalted butter, melted

Pinch of kosher salt

½ teaspoon maple extract

I come from the desert region of Southern California. But living in New England for as long as I did, it was hard for me not to adopt the lifestyle there and feel like I truly belonged in that environment. These cheesecake bars perfectly capture my experience of living in New England, where fall is queen and maple syrup flows like a second bloodstream.

The topping on these bars resembles the classic old-timey ice cream topping known as wet nuts. It gives the cheesecake a beautiful marbled maple color and amplifies the maple flavor. For the best taste, let these bars chill in the fridge for a while—the longer, the better, as the flavors develop and become even more delicious.

1. Preheat the oven to 350°F. Spray a 9-by-9-inch (or 8-by-8-inch) pan with baking spray and line with parchment paper. Set aside. Fill a heatproof casserole dish or pan two-thirds full with water and place it in the center of the bottom rack of the oven.

2. Make the crust. In a small bowl, whisk together the graham cracker crumbs, sugar, and salt. Add the butter and mix it with a fork until the mixture looks like wet beach sand, using the fork to break up any large clumps.

3. Pour the mixture into the prepared pan and press it into an even layer. Bake for 10 minutes; the crust will darken. Remove and cool completely on a wire rack.

4. Meanwhile, make the cheesecake filling. In a food processor, add the cream cheese, sugar, maple syrup, eggs, vanilla extract, maple extract, and half-and-half. Pulse until fully incorporated and smooth, stopping a few

times and scraping down the sides and bottom with a rubber spatula. Pour the mixture over the cooled crust and smooth it into an even layer. Bake for 15 minutes.

5 While the cheesecake bakes, make the topping. Roughly chop the walnuts and place them into a small bowl. Add the maple syrup, brown sugar, butter, salt, and maple extract and stir until evenly combined.

6 After the cheesecake has baked for 15 minutes, carefully remove it from the oven; the top should be slightly set. With a tablespoon, carefully spoon the maple-walnut topping sporadically over the top of the cheesecake, making sure not to drop the topping, causing it to sink into the cheesecake. Return to the oven and bake for another 30 to 35 minutes, or until the edges are set and the center slightly jiggles, like gelatin.

7 Turn off the oven, crack open the oven door slightly, and let the cheesecake cool inside the warm oven, which will prevent cracking. It will puff up and slowly deflate as it cools.

8 Once cooled, cover the pan with foil and refrigerate for at least 2 hours; it is best to cool overnight. Portion into squares and serve.

Note: This method creates steam in the oven, which helps prevent the cheesecake from cracking, produces an even bake, and helps create a creamy center.

SCOTCHEROOS

6 cups (180 g) rice cereal
1 cup (330 g) light corn syrup
¾ cup (150 g) granulated sugar
¼ cup (55 g) light brown sugar
1½ cups (420 g) crunchy peanut butter or (375 g) creamy peanut butter
1½ teaspoons vanilla extract
1 teaspoon kosher salt
One 12-ounce bag dark chocolate chips
One 11-ounce bag butterscotch chips
Flaky sea salt for garnish

When I decided to write this cookbook, this was one of the first recipes I jotted down. If you've never tried scotcheroos, you've probably at least heard of their flavor combo: peanut butter, chocolate, and butterscotch. It's surprising how well these three flavors complement each other, and they combine to create this unique salty-sweet treat.

The bars are made with crispy rice cereal mixed with melted peanut butter and then pressed into a pan. Once they've set, you top them with a chocolate-butterscotch coating—that's usually all there is to it. But I do a few things differently. I swap the creamy peanut butter for crunchy to add some texture, because the rice cereal loses its crunch when mixed with melted peanut butter and compressed in a pan. To tone down the sweetness, I use dark chocolate. And to ramp up the salty-sweet contrast, I sprinkle flaky sea salt on top of the coating. And that's it!

1. Spray a 9-by-13-inch pan with baking spray and line with parchment paper, then spray the parchment. Set aside.
2. In a large bowl add the rice cereal. Set aside.
3. In a medium saucepan over medium-low heat, add the corn syrup and sugars. Stirring occasionally, bring the mixture to just a boil, making sure the sugars are dissolved and combined. Turn off the heat and stir in the peanut butter, vanilla, and salt until melted and evenly combined.
4. Carefully pour the hot peanut butter mixture over the rice cereal and with a wooden spoon, stir to evenly combine and coat the cereal.

5 Pour the cereal mixture into the prepared pan, spread into an even layer, and let cool.

6 Meanwhile, add the chocolate chips and butterscotch chips to a heatproof bowl. Microwave in 30-second intervals, stirring in between until melted and evenly combined. Pour the chocolate-butterscotch mixture over the cereal layer and spread evenly. Garnish with flaky salt. Let cool completely before serving.

Potlucks can happen anywhere—embrace the setting, savor the company, and make memories to treasure.

BUMPY ROAD CEREAL BARS

- 2 cups (110 g) mini marshmallows
- 1 cup (175 g) dark chocolate chips
- 9 cups (270 g) cocoa rice cereal
- ½ cup (113 g) unsalted butter
- One 24-ounce bag large marshmallows
- 2 teaspoons kosher salt
- 1 teaspoon vanilla extract
- 1 cup (140 g) lightly salted almonds, toasted and chopped
- One 7-ounce jar marshmallow creme

I remember losing a tooth while munching on rocky road fudge when I was in middle school. It turns out I still had a baby tooth to lose! I was at the mall, and it was quite the moment of panic, thinking I had lost an adult tooth. I was also annoyed that the fudge was tough enough to cause an incident like that. I buried that memory for a while, which was probably my way of coping with that embarrassing middle school moment at the mall.

But then, I remembered that experience when my son Jasper asked for rocky road ice cream (or as he calls it, bumpy road). I decided that if a confectionery at the mall couldn't make a rocky road–inspired snack soft enough so that it wouldn't break a tooth, I would. So, I ditched the fudge and went for a cereal bar as a soft base to balance out the hard mix-ins. The best part is layering marshmallow creme in between, which really amps up the marshmallow flavor and makes a more flexible bar. And in honor of Jasper, rocky road will forever be known as bumpy road.

1. Place the mini marshmallows and chocolate chips in a bowl and place in the freezer until ready to use. (See the baking tip that follows.)

2. Spray a 9-by-13-inch pan with baking spray and line with parchment paper, leaving an overhang over the long sides of the pan. Set aside.

3. In a large bowl, add the cocoa cereal and set aside.

4. In a large saucepan over medium heat, add the butter. Melt the butter, swirling the pan occasionally to evenly distribute the browning and to prevent the butter from burning. Once melted, the butter will begin to foam up; at this point, lower the heat to medium-low and continue

Bumpy Road Cereal Bars travel well! Just cut and store, stacking layers between parchment paper to prevent sticking.

to brown, occasionally swirling the pan. The crackling will start to lower, and the foam will decrease. At this point, watch the center of the foam; once the center begins to turn a golden, nutty color, swirl the pan evenly and, once evenly golden, remove the pan from the heat.

5 Remove the mini marshmallows and chocolate chips from the freezer.

6 Add the large marshmallows to the brown butter and with a wooden spoon, stir constantly until the marshmallows melt. Add the salt and vanilla and stir to combine.

7 Carefully pour the hot butter-marshmallow mixture over the cocoa cereal and with the wooden spoon, fold together until some of the cereal is partially coated. Move fast, as soon as the mixture cools the harder it is to stir.

8 Once the cereal is partially coated, add the almonds, mini marshmallows, and chocolate chips and fold until evenly combined.

9 Transfer half of the cereal mixture to the prepared pan and press firmly into an even layer. Add the marshmallow creme on top and spread. Don't worry if it's not even; you don't need every bite to have marshmallow creme. Add the remaining cereal mixture and press firmly into an even layer. Let cool and set for at least 1 hour before slicing into portions.

BAKING TIP:
KEEP IT COOL

Consider using your freezer as an extension of your kitchen's counter space for optimal baking results. This is especially helpful when working with ingredients that require temperature control, such as cubed butter for pie dough or crumble toppings for crisps, both of which bake better when ice cold.

By utilizing your freezer, you can get ahead in your baking process while ensuring that ingredients stay chilled as needed, rather than risking them reaching room temperature prematurely. This is particularly useful when incorporating items into a hot mixture, as it helps to prevent them from melting too quickly so that they maintain the desired texture.

For example, when making cereal treat bars, the residual heat from the hot marshmallow mixture can quickly melt chocolate chips and mini marshmallows. However, using your freezer strategically, you can keep these ingredients solid, allowing for better texture and distinct flavors in every bite.

BANANA FUDGE SNACKING CAKE

FOR THE CAKE

1¾ cups (218 g) all-purpose flour

1 teaspoon baking powder

½ teaspoon baking soda

½ teaspoon kosher salt

½ cup (120 g) sour cream

½ cup (120 g) whole milk

½ cup (113 g) unsalted butter, softened

1 cup (200 g) granulated sugar

2 eggs

1 teaspoon vanilla extract

3 ripe bananas, mashed

FOR THE FUDGE FROSTING

½ cup (113 g) unsalted butter

½ cup (120 g) whole milk

½ cup (100 g) granulated sugar

1 cup (175 g) dark chocolate chips

1 teaspoon vanilla extract

Sometimes, a simple cake is all you need. When I stumbled upon this recipe in my husband's family cookbook, I thought it was for a fudgy chocolate banana cake. But it turned out to be something even better. This cake is all about the bananas, with just a hint of vanilla and no other spices. It's a refreshing change from the usual banana bakes loaded with warm spices. The banana flavor shines through in this cake and is moderately sweet. A bit nostalgic and utterly delicious, it's topped with a fudgy frosting that never sets. The original recipe didn't call it a snacking cake, but after watching my husband make multiple "trips" to the kitchen for another slice, I realized we had a snacking cake on our hands.

1. Preheat your oven to 350°F and spray a 9-by-13-inch pan with baking spray. Set aside.
2. Make the cake. In a medium bowl, whisk together the flour, baking powder, baking soda, and salt until evenly combined.
3. In a small bowl, whisk together the sour cream and milk. Set aside.
4. In a separate medium bowl with an electric hand mixer, cream together the butter and sugar until light and fluffy, 2 to 3 minutes. Stop the mixer and add the eggs and vanilla. Mix until well combined, about 1 minute. Stop the mixer and add the bananas; mix until just combined.

5 Add half the dry ingredients to the wet ingredients and mix until just combined. Then add half the sour cream-milk mixture and mix. Repeat alternating until just combined; don't overmix.

6 Pour the batter into the prepared pan and bake for 25 to 30 minutes, or until a toothpick or cake tester inserted in the middle comes out clean. Place on a wire rack and let cool.

7 Meanwhile, make the fudge frosting. In a medium saucepan over medium heat, add the butter, milk, and sugar. Occasionally stir until melted and combined and sugar is dissolved. Bring to just a boil. Remove from the heat and stir in the chocolate chips and vanilla until melted, smooth, and shiny.

8 Pour the hot frosting over the warm cake and spread evenly. Let the cake completely cool before serving.

BAKING TIP:
BE MINDFUL OF FROZEN BANANAS

If you're anything like me, you often buy bananas but never quite get around to eating them all before they turn brown and mushy. Rather than tossing them out, you can toss them in the freezer with the other forgotten banana bunches.

Those frozen bananas come in handy when a craving for banana bread strikes or a recipe calls for ripe bananas. However, there are a few things to remember when baking with frozen bananas.

It's crucial to drain peeled frozen bananas after thawing to remove excess liquid. Freezing causes bananas to release moisture, which can affect the texture and consistency of baked goods. Draining helps prevent your baked goods from becoming too dense or soggy, ensuring a better overall texture.

It's also worth noting that frozen bananas can develop a slightly fermented flavor if stored for a long time. Freezing can break down the cell walls of the banana, allowing enzymes to interact with the fruit's sugars, resulting in a more pronounced flavor change over time. To minimize this effect, it's best to use frozen bananas within a few months of freezing.

Here's a timeline for using frozen bananas:

1 TO 2 MONTHS: Perfectly fine, with a more pronounced banana flavor.

2 TO 4 MONTHS: Some fermentation has started, giving them a bananas Foster flavor.

4-PLUS MONTHS: It's best to toss them out at this point.

CHAPTER TWO

SHEET PANS

I'm intrigued by the trend in home cooking toward sheet pan meals, often hailed as "easy," "simple," and perfect for a "quick weeknight meal." While this may be true, sheet pan baking, beyond cookies, requires a bit more creativity and ventures beyond the traditional baking realm. While most recipes baked on a sheet pan could easily be made in a 9-by-13-inch or larger pan, opting for a sheet pan means stepping away from the familiar and embracing an entirely new baking experience.

For example, baking cookie dough as bars creates a denser, chewier texture with crisp, caramelized edges and a soft, chewy center. Cakes baked on a sheet pan serve more people, have a more even crumb, and achieve a better frosting-to-cake ratio. For pies and tarts, a sheet pan ensures a crisper, more evenly baked crust, minimizes the risk of raw or undercooked dough, and prevents the crust from burning before the center is fully cooked due to the even distribution of filling to crust.

One concern with sheet pan baking is the possibility that the edges are not tall enough, which could lead to spills. Additionally, converting from a traditional baking pan to a sheet pan often requires doubling the recipe or adjusting ratios to ensure everything fits appropriately. Each dessert baked on a sheet pan is a testament to creativity and resourcefulness, showcasing our willingness to take risks and tackle challenges head-on, opting for the less conventional path.

With their expansive surface area, sheet pans have served as the canvas for some of my most ambitious potluck creations. From delicate cookies to elaborate slab pies, these pans have witnessed the evolution of my baking skills and the expansion of my dessert repertoire. When I look at a recipe, I often wonder, "Could this be made on a sheet pan?" I'm open to the idea that tradition can be reimagined and that we can break the rules to introduce something new, unexpected, and hopefully embraced.

BROWN BUTTER SNICKERDOODLE COOKIE BARS

FOR THE COOKIE

1 cup (227 g) unsalted butter
2½ cups (312 g) all-purpose flour
1 teaspoon baking soda
½ teaspoon kosher salt
2 teaspoons cream of tartar
1½ teaspoons ground cinnamon
1 cup (200 g) granulated sugar
½ cup (110 g) light brown sugar
2 teaspoons vanilla extract
2 eggs plus 1 yolk

FOR THE COATING

⅓ cup (66 g) granulated sugar
1½ teaspoons ground cinnamon

A snickerdoodle is my cookie of comfort. Rolled in cinnamon sugar and baked, it creates a satisfying contrast of crispy edges and a chewy center. Despite its simple ingredients, individually rolling each cookie in cinnamon and sugar can be time-consuming, especially when you're making a lot of them for a potluck. So I decided to bake them on a sheet pan to make cookie bars. But I don't stop there. I brown the butter to enhance the warm, buttery flavors and add a subtle nuttiness to complement the cinnamon. I even increase the amount of cinnamon in the batter. Browning butter may sound fancy, but it's simple and requires minimal effort with significant results. However, I must warn you that once you try a brown butter snickerdoodle, your view of the classic cookie might be forever changed.

1 Make the cookie. In a medium saucepan over medium heat, add the butter. Melt the butter, swirling the pan occasionally to evenly distribute the browning and prevent the butter from browning too quickly. Once melted, the butter will begin to foam up; at this point, lower the heat to medium-low and continue to brown, occasionally swirling the pan. The crackling will start to lower, and the foam will decrease. At this point, watch the center of the foam; once the center begins to turn a golden, nutty color, swirl the pan evenly and, once evenly golden, remove the pan from the heat. Pour the brown butter into a small heatproof bowl through a fine mesh sieve. Set aside and let cool.

continues →

2. Spray a 9½-by-13½-inch sheet pan with baking spray, then line with parchment paper, leaving an overhang on two sides of the pan. Spray the parchment paper with baking spray and set aside.
3. In a medium bowl, whisk together the flour, baking soda, salt, cream of tartar, and ground cinnamon until evenly combined.
4. In a separate medium bowl, add the granulated sugar, brown sugar, and vanilla extract. Whisk to combine. Add the eggs and yolk and whisk vigorously until combined and the mixture is a khaki color and frothy.
5. Slowly pour the brown butter into the sugar mixture while whisking continuously until combined.
6. Add the flour mixture and fold together with a wooden spoon until fully combined and no visible flour streaks appear. The dough will be very stiff.
7. Dump the dough onto the prepared pan and flatten out the dough to evenly spread. Cover lightly in plastic wrap and chill in the refrigerator for at least 30 minutes but no longer than 1 hour.
8. Meanwhile, mix the coating for the cookie. In a small bowl, whisk together the granulated sugar and ground cinnamon. Set aside. Preheat the oven to 350° F.
9. Once the dough is chilled, remove the plastic wrap and pour the cinnamon-sugar mixture onto the dough. Pick up the pan and tilt it in different directions to evenly coat the cookie with the cinnamon-sugar mixture. Once fully coated, discard any excess mixture.
10. Bake for 20 to 25 minutes until the dough puffs up and the top appears dry. Cool on a wire rack. Let the cookie bar cool completely to room temperature before cutting. Cutting while hot will push the warm dough together and make a dense, wet cookie rather than a chewy cookie.

BAKING TIP: BROWNING BUTTER ISN'T THAT SCARY

Brown butter is your secret weapon for next-level baked goods! It adds a rich, nutty flavor that regular butter just can't match. Imagine taking your cookies, cakes, and frosting from good to "OMG, what's in this?!"—that's the power of browned butter.

It's easy to make, too! Just melt butter in a saucepan over medium heat, swirling occasionally for even cooking. Watch the butter closely as it starts to foam—it can go from beautifully browned to burnt quickly. Once the foam settles and the butter turns a golden brown with a nutty aroma, it's ready. A trick I learned was to watch the center of the foam: When it starts to turn golden brown, that's the cue it's about done. The foaming will subside, indicating that brown butter perfection has been reached. For super smooth butter, strain it through a fine mesh sieve to catch any burnt bits.

The best part? You can make brown butter ahead of time! After cooling to room temperature, store it in an airtight container in the fridge for up to two weeks. When you're ready to bake, let it warm to room temperature for that special touch in all your baking adventures.

Browning butter is a game changer—once you try it, you'll be hooked!

WHOLE WHEAT CHOCOLATE CHIP COOKIE BARS WITH SALTED VANILLA FROSTING

FOR THE COOKIE BAR

- 1 cup (120 g) whole wheat flour
- 1 cup (125 g) all-purpose flour
- 1 teaspoon baking soda
- 1½ teaspoons baking powder
- ½ teaspoon kosher salt
- 1 cup (227 g) salted butter, room temperature
- ½ cup (100 g) granulated sugar
- ¾ cup (165 g) dark brown sugar, lightly packed
- 2 eggs
- ½ teaspoon vanilla extract
- ¼ teaspoon almond extract
- 1 cup (175 g) dark chocolate chips
- ½ cup (88 g) milk chocolate chips

FOR THE VANILLA FROSTING

- 1 cup (227 g) salted butter, room temperature
- 1¼ cups (141 g) powdered sugar
- 1 teaspoon vanilla extract
- 1 tablespoon heavy whipping cream

Is there such a thing as the perfect chocolate chip cookie? It's a question that can ignite passionate debates. Some prefer them buttery with just a hint of chocolate, while others crave a crispy texture or a chewy center. People argue about the best sugar or blend of sugars; some even debate the type of chocolate to include. The discussions can seem endless, with new variations and cookie identities constantly emerging. Do you see where I'm going with this?

So instead of claiming the perfect chocolate chip cookie recipe, I offer my take on it—a slightly saltier, crowd-pleasing recipe for those who appreciate the cookie's versatility.

In this recipe, both the cookie and frosting use salted butter—yes, salted butter! It might sound unconventional in today's unsalted butter world, but the adjusted sugar ratios create a beautifully balanced salty-sweet cookie with an irresistible allure. I suggest adding a dollop of frosting to the center of each portioned bar, but feel free to go all out with frosting from end to end if that's your style.

1. Spray a 9½-by-13½-inch sheet pan with baking spray, then line with parchment paper, leaving an overhang on the long sides of the pan. Spray the parchment paper with baking spray and set aside.

2. Make the cookie bar. In a medium bowl, whisk together the whole wheat flour, all-purpose flour, baking soda, baking powder, and salt until combined. Set aside.

continues

3 In a separate medium bowl, blend together the butter, sugar, and dark brown sugar with a hand mixer with the beater attachments on medium-high speed until creamy and smooth—about 5 minutes.

4 Stop the mixer and add the eggs and the vanilla and almond extracts. Blend together on medium speed until incorporated—about 1 minute.

5 Stop the mixer and add the flour mixture. Blend together on medium speed until just combined; there will be a few visible flour streaks.

6 Add the dark and milk chocolates. With a wooden spoon, fold in the chocolate by hand until the chocolate is evenly distributed and no visible flour shows, making sure to scrape the sides and bottom of the bowl.

7 Scrape the cookie dough onto the prepared sheet pan and evenly spread it using the back of a wooden spoon or an offset spatula. Cover tightly with plastic wrap and let chill in the refrigerator for at least 1 hour or overnight.

8 Before baking, position an oven rack in the center of the oven and preheat to 350°F .

9 Remove the dough from the refrigerator and discard the plastic wrap. Bake for 20 to 25 minutes, or until the cookie is evenly golden brown and slightly puffy when you touch the center of the cookie. Remove from the oven and cool completely on a wire rack.

10 While the cookie cools, make the frosting. In a medium bowl, blend together the butter and powdered sugar with a hand mixer with the beater attachments on medium-high speed until creamy and smooth—about 5 minutes.

11 Stop the mixer and add the vanilla extract and heavy whipping cream. Return the mixer to medium speed and blend together until fluffy and smooth—about 1 minute.

12 Once the cookie is cooled completely, frost the cookie bar as desired. I prefer scoring and portioning the large cookie into bars, leaving the bars on the pan, and using a teaspoon to dollop frosting in the middle. Then, with the back of the spoon, pull it down and toward you to make a teardrop swoosh.

BAKING TIP: GIVE IT A CHILL

Chilling your cookie dough for at least 30 minutes before baking works wonders in two ways. First, it gives the ingredients a chance to mingle, amplifying your cookies' overall flavor and complexity. Second, it works wonders for texture. When the fat in the dough is colder, it takes longer to spread out during baking. This results in a thicker, chewier cookie that's just irresistible.

And here's a bonus: This trick isn't just for individual cookies. It works like a charm for sheet pan cookies, too. Chilling the dough helps the cookie bake more slowly and evenly, preventing it from getting too crispy around the edges before the center is fully baked.

BAKED GOODS

IN THE summer of 2003, a new adventure began for me as I headed to Boston, Massachusetts. It came about after I'd found myself swept up in a whirlwind romance with a boy back home in California. It felt like fate. But his path was leading him to Berklee College of Music in Boston, so after only three weeks of dating, I took a leap of faith, selling all my belongings and heading out with only $1,000 to follow him. Little did I know this move would place me amid a pivotal moment in Massachusetts history.

In 2003, the Massachusetts Supreme Judicial Court overturned the ban on same-sex marriage, sparking a fierce battle for marriage equality. My boyfriend and I dove headfirst into this movement, joining rallies outside the statehouse where we stood tall despite facing hateful opposition.

Those early rallies, though emotionally draining, were also incredibly empowering. They gave us a sense of unity and purpose that went beyond our relationship. We felt part of something historic, part of a larger community fighting for equality.

As the fight continued, we unintentionally became symbols of the movement when a national camera crew captured our kiss in the face of bigotry, thrusting us into the spotlight overnight. Sud-

FOR EQUALITY

denly, we were seen as a representation of modern-day love, a symbol of strength and defiance.

But our involvement was about more than just us. It was about standing up for the rights of the entire LGBTQIA+ community. That's why when the opportunity arose to intern with MassEquality in 2006, I jumped at it. That summer, surrounded by passionate individuals, I witnessed the power of collective action.

Our days were packed with meetings, rallies, and press conferences, but the real magic happened during breaks. Gathered around a table filled with homemade baked goods, we found comfort in each other's company amid the chaos of the fight.

Food was always part of those moments, from pizza to an array of baked treats like chocolate chip cookies, magic bars, lemon bars, snacking cakes, and pies. These simple, nostalgic desserts gave us the energy and comfort we needed during our tireless work.

Looking back, those summers were transformative, filled with lifelong friendships, lessons in resilience, and a newfound passion for advocacy. Whenever I grab a grab-and-go baked good, I'm reminded of the strength and resilience of my community.

A TALE OF PETER

IT'S PRETTY unsettling to think about how queer history has been pushed to the sidelines, barely a whisper in the grand story of written records. The little we have about our lives, fights, and victories over time drives home how our stories have been brushed aside. Seeing our rich history of resilience and strength dismissed as inappropriate and not worthy is heartbreaking.

But in this gloomy picture, there's a glimmer of hope—a light showing us how to take back our story. So many people are working tirelessly to rewrite our narrative, show how our community intersects with so many others, and finally, give us the recognition we've always deserved.

Before my time in Massachusetts and working with MassEquality, my understanding of my community was painfully narrow. My knowledge was clouded by twisted facts and distorted views spread by the media and conservative religious beliefs. However, my internship at MassEquality changed everything.

I had the honor of meeting incredible individuals, some in their twilight years, who had dedicated their lives to fighting for acceptance, equality, and the right to love freely. These were the voices of Stonewall, the allies of Harvey Milk, the heroes of AIDS clinics, and the survivors of the Lavender Scare. Their stories, told with raw emotion and unshakable conviction, reshaped my view of equality and filled me with deep gratitude.

One person who stands out is Peter, a man in his late 80s living on Cape Cod. Peter survived the Stonewall riots and was the last of his chosen family lost to AIDS. His strength, resilience, and unwavering dedication to our community left a lasting impression on me. Our talks on his porch recounting our community's history over coffee and butterscotch oatmeal cookies, a recipe he cherished from his late partner, showed me our history's depth and breadth.

These butterscotch oatmeal cookie bars aren't just for Peter; they're a symbol of the enduring legacy of queer history. Whether written down or spoken from one person to another, our history is real, it's profound, and it will last.

OATMEAL BUTTERSCOTCH COOKIE BARS

- 1½ cups (187 g) all-purpose flour
- 3 cups (270 g) old-fashioned oats
- 1 teaspoon baking soda
- 1 teaspoon baking powder
- 2 teaspoons kosher salt
- 1½ teaspoons ground cinnamon
- ½ teaspoon ground nutmeg
- ¼ teaspoon ground ginger
- 1 cup (227 g) unsalted butter, softened
- ½ cup (100 g) granulated sugar
- 1 cup (220 g) light brown sugar
- 2 eggs
- 2 tablespoons molasses
- 1 teaspoon vanilla extract
- One 11-ounce bag butterscotch chips

This recipe came from my friend Peter's late partner. It isn't his exact recipe; still, after enjoying plenty of them that summer in 2006, I've come quite close, with the help of my food memory. These bars are robust with oats, yet they are delicately balanced. Their rich molasses flavor is complemented by the butterscotch being a key player, which is subtle enough to take the cookies from good to absolutely irresistible without overshadowing the other flavors. I did my best to capture those flavors here, and I think Peter would approve.

1. Preheat your oven to 350° F and spray a 9½-by-13½-inch sheet pan with baking spray and line with parchment paper, leaving an overhang over the longest edges. Spray the parchment with baking spray. Set aside.
2. In a medium bowl, whisk together the flour, oats, baking soda, baking powder, salt, cinnamon, nutmeg, and ginger until evenly combined. Set aside.
3. In a separate medium bowl with an electric hand mixer, cream the butter and sugars together until light and fluffy, 2 to 3 minutes. Stop the mixer and add the eggs, molasses, and vanilla and mix until combined, about 1 minute.

continues

4. Add the dry ingredients to the wet ingredients and mix on medium-low speed until just combined, with a few visible flour streaks. With a wooden spoon, fold in the butterscotch chips until evenly combined.
5. Pour the dough into the prepared pan and spread evenly. Chill in the refrigerator for at least 30 minutes.
6. Bake for 20 to 25 minutes, or until the cookie is golden brown and puffed up. Cool completely on a wire rack before portioning.

CARAMEL APPLE PIE BARS

FOR THE CRUST

1 cup (227 g) unsalted butter, room temperature

½ cup (100 g) granulated sugar

2 cups (250 g) all-purpose flour

¼ teaspoon kosher salt

FOR THE APPLE FILLING

4 to 5 apples, peeled, cored, and chopped (about 4 cups)

½ cup (100 g) granulated sugar

1 teaspoon ground cinnamon

¼ teaspoon ground nutmeg

¼ teaspoon kosher salt

Juice of 1 lemon

2 tablespoons cornstarch

FOR THE CARAMEL TOPPING

One 14-ounce can sweetened condensed milk

½ cup (110 g) light brown sugar

¼ cup (82 g) light corn syrup

1 teaspoon vanilla extract

Pinch of kosher salt

After my wake-up call to the world of political activism, the idea of being as "American as apple pie" suddenly seemed like a shallow cliché. Were we really as humble as that saying suggests? It seemed like a facade, masking the complexities of our society and culture. These caramel apple pie bars are my way of baking my values into a dessert. The slightly salty shortbread crust, spiced apple filling, and messy caramel topping represent our world's imperfect yet delightful nature. I purposely leave the caramel topping uneven, showing that I value authenticity over perfection. It's a reminder that embracing our "imperfections" and truths is more important than trying to cover them up for the sake of fitting in.

1. Preheat your oven to 350° F and spray a 9½-by-13½-inch sheet pan with baking spray and line with parchment paper, leaving an overhang over the longest edges. Spray the parchment. Set aside.
2. Make the crust. In a medium bowl with an electric hand mixer, cream together the butter and sugar until light and fluffy. Add the flour and salt and mix until crumbly.
3. Press the mixture into the bottom of the prepared pan to form an even layer. Bake the crust for 15 to 20 minutes, until lightly golden brown. Remove from the oven and let it cool slightly.
4. Meanwhile, prepare the apple filling. In a large bowl, combine the apples, sugar, cinnamon, nutmeg, salt, lemon juice, and cornstarch. With your hands, toss together until the apples are evenly coated. Pour the apple mixture onto the crust and spread evenly. Bake for 15 minutes.

continues →

5 Meanwhile, prepare the caramel topping. In a medium saucepan over medium-low heat, add the condensed milk, brown sugar, corn syrup, vanilla, and salt. With a wooden spoon, constantly stir until the sugar is melted and the mixture is evenly combined and smooth. Bring to just a boil and remove from the heat. Pour the mixture through a fine mesh sieve over a heatproof bowl to collect any burnt sugary pieces.

6 Pour the caramel over the apple layer and continue baking for 20 to 25 minutes, rotating the pan halfway through. The top will puff around the edges first, then continue puffing toward the center. Remove from the oven when the bars are evenly puffed, golden brown, and the tops look dry. Cool on a wire rack. Once cooled, loosely cover in plastic wrap and chill in the refrigerator for at least 1 hour to continue firming up before portioning and serving.

JAMMY COCONUT CHESS SQUARES

FOR THE CRUST

1 cup (227 g) unsalted butter, softened

½ cup (100 g) granulated sugar

2 cups (250 g) all-purpose flour

¼ teaspoon kosher salt

FOR THE CUSTARD FILLING

1 cup (227 g) unsalted butter, melted

1½ cups (300 g) granulated sugar

4 eggs

1 teaspoon vanilla extract

1 teaspoon coconut extract

¼ teaspoon kosher salt

1 cup (125 g) all-purpose flour

½ cup (125 g) canned coconut milk

2 cups (160 g) shredded sweetened coconut

½ cup (160 g) jam of choice

Moving to the South brought plenty of pleasant surprises—turns out, it's not all doom and gloom down here. One delightful discovery was chess pie, a simple yet delicious custard pie with a slightly crisp and caramelized top. And, as with most pies, you can find it in bar form, too.

While some chess pie recipes use cornmeal, this one sticks with flour. I ramp up the coconut flavor by adding shredded coconut, canned coconut milk, and coconut extract to the filling. Then I top the bars with preserves for a pop of acidity and color. You can use any preserves you like, but my go-to is whatever seasonal preserves my husband has just canned. Strawberries are always a winner in my book.

1. Preheat your oven to 350° F and spray a 9½-by-13½-inch sheet pan with baking spray and line with parchment paper, leaving an overhang over the longest edges. Spray the parchment. Set aside.
2. Make the crust. In a medium bowl with an electric hand mixer, cream together the butter and sugar until light and fluffy. Add the flour and salt and mix until crumbly.
3. Press the mixture into the bottom of the prepared pan to form an even layer. Bake the crust for 15 to 20 minutes until lightly golden brown. Remove from the oven and let it cool slightly.

Jammy Coconut Chess Squares are a treat for breakfast or brunch—especially when served warm.

4 Meanwhile, make the custard filling. In a medium bowl with an electric hand mixer, beat together the butter and sugar until combined, 1 to 2 minutes. Stop the mixer and add the eggs and the vanilla and coconut extracts and mix until combined, about 1 minute.

5 Stop the mixer and add the salt and flour and mix until just combined, about 1 minute. Stop the mixer and add the coconut milk and shredded coconut and mix until just combined.

6 Pour the custard onto the crust and spread evenly. Dollop jam randomly over the custard and with a butter knife, carefully swirl the jam through the custard, making sure to keep the jam on top and not sinking to the bottom. Bake for 30 to 40 minutes, or until the center is slightly jiggly and the bars have puffed up and lightly golden brown. Cool completely on a wire rack before portioning.

LEMON-THYME BARS

FOR THE CRUST

- 1 cup (227 g) unsalted butter, softened
- ½ cup (100 g) granulated sugar
- 2 cups (250 g) all-purpose flour
- ½ teaspoon kosher salt
- 1 tablespoon fresh thyme leaves, finely chopped

FOR THE LEMON CURD

- 4 eggs plus 1 egg yolk
- 1 cup (200 g) granulated sugar
- 1 cup (250 g) lemon juice, 4 to 6 lemons
- ½ cup (113 g) unsalted butter
- 1 tablespoon heavy whipping cream
- 1¼ teaspoons kosher salt
- 1 teaspoon vanilla extract
- Zest of 1 lemon
- Powdered sugar for dusting

Lemon bars are a true delight—bright, buttery, and just the right balance of tangy and sweet. With a buttery shortbread crust as the foundation, these bars are topped with a golden, firm lemon curd that adds a chewy, soft texture. A dusting of powdered sugar on top adds a touch of sweetness, making them a sought-after treat during the spring and summer months.

But why stop at traditional lemon bars? As a pastry chef, I love experimenting with flavors to create new and exciting desserts. Adding fresh thyme is one of my favorite twists on the classic lemon bar. Thyme's natural hint of lemon pairs beautifully with the citrusy flavors of the bars. I mix fresh thyme into the shortbread crust, allowing its flavors to infuse the buttery base during baking. I also boost the citrus content in the lemon curd to ensure a vibrant, zesty flavor. The result? A refreshing and unique take on lemon bars that is sure to become a new favorite.

1. Preheat your oven to 350° F and spray a 9½-by-13½-inch quarter sheet pan with baking spray and line with parchment paper, leaving an overhang along the edges. Spray the parchment.
2. Make the crust. In a large mixing bowl, cream together the softened butter and granulated sugar until light and fluffy.
3. Add the flour, salt, and thyme leaves to the butter mixture. Mix until the dough comes together and forms a crumbly texture.
4. Press the dough evenly into the bottom of the prepared baking pan.

5. Bake the crust in the preheated oven for 20 to 25 minutes, or until lightly golden brown.
6. While the crust is baking, prepare the lemon curd filling. In a medium bowl, whisk together the eggs, yolk, and granulated sugar until well combined. Set aside.
7. In a medium saucepan, over medium-low heat, add lemon juice, butter, and heavy whipping cream and bring to just a boil and the butter is melted.
8. Remove from heat and slowly pour the hot lemon mixture into the sugar-egg mixture while constantly whisking vigorously until combined. Return the lemon-egg mixture back to the saucepan and return to medium-low heat.
9. With a wooden spoon, continuously stir the lemon-egg mixture, making sure to scrape the sides and bottom of the saucepan, until thickened but not boiling, about 2 to 4 minutes.
10. Remove from heat and pass through a fine mesh sieve over a heatproof bowl. Stir in the salt, vanilla extract, and lemon zest.
11. Pour the lemon filling over the hot crust, then return the pan to the oven.
12. Bake for an additional 20 to 25 minutes, or until the filling is set and the edges are lightly golden brown.
13. Allow the lemon bars to cool completely in the pan on a wire rack.
14. Once cooled, dust the top with powdered sugar. Cut into squares and serve.

OATMEAL FUDGE BARS

FOR THE BARS

- 1 cup (227 g) unsalted butter, softened
- 1 cup (200 g) light brown sugar
- 1 teaspoon vanilla extract
- 1½ cups (187 g) all-purpose flour
- 1 teaspoon baking soda
- 1 teaspoon ground cinnamon
- ½ teaspoon kosher salt
- 2 cups (180 g) old-fashioned oats

FOR THE CHOCOLATE FILLING

- One 14-ounce can sweetened condensed milk
- One 12-ounce bag semi-sweet chocolate chips
- 2 tablespoons unsalted butter
- ½ teaspoon kosher salt
- 1 teaspoon vanilla extract

Oatmeal chocolate chip cookies were a regular treat when I was growing up. They had this light hint of cinnamon and were loaded with chocolate chips—soft and chewy in the middle with those irresistible crispy edges. I never got a peek at the recipe, but I can still perfectly recall the taste and the irresistible aroma. These bars are my take on that cherished family recipe, passed down only through memory. Instead of scattering chocolate chips throughout, I've sandwiched fudge between layers of oatmeal cookie dough and baked them into bars.

1. Preheat your oven to 350° F, spray a 9½-by-13½-inch sheet pan with baking spray, then line it with parchment paper. Set aside.
2. In a medium bowl with an electric hand mixer, cream together the butter, brown sugar, and vanilla extract until smooth.
3. In a medium bowl, whisk together the flour, baking soda, cinnamon, and salt.
4. With the electric hand mixer on medium-low speed, gradually add the dry ingredients to the butter mixture, mixing until just combined. Stop the mixer and with a rubber spatula, fold in the oats until evenly distributed. Set aside.
5. Make the chocolate filling. In a medium saucepan, combine the sweetened condensed milk, chocolate chips, butter, salt, and vanilla. Cook over low heat, stirring constantly, until the chocolate chips are melted and the mixture is smooth and shiny.

6. Press half of the oat mixture into the bottom of the prepared pan, forming an even layer. Pour the chocolate mixture over the oat layer and spread into an even layer. Crumble the remaining oat mixture evenly over the chocolate layer.
7. Bake for 25 to 30 minutes, or until the top is golden brown.
8. Set the bars on a wire rack and cool completely in the pan before cutting into bars.

PULL-APART STRAWBERRY SHORTCAKE

FOR THE STRAWBERRIES

1 pound strawberries
½ cup (110 g) light brown sugar

FOR THE BISCUITS

4 cups (500 g) all-purpose flour
2 teaspoons kosher salt
1 tablespoon plus 1 teaspoon baking powder
½ teaspoon baking soda
½ cup (100 g) vegetable oil
2 cups (480 g) buttermilk
½ cup (100 g) granulated sugar
2 tablespoons unsalted butter, melted
Sugar in the raw for coating

FOR THE WHIPPED CREAM TOPPING

One 8-ounce package mascarpone
1 cup (113 g) powdered sugar
Zest of 1 lemon
Pinch of kosher salt
1 cup (240 g) heavy whipping cream

This recipe came to me when I was learning the art of making biscuits, after moving to the South. I quickly learned the importance of placing biscuits close together on the sheet pan so they rise together, creating those perfect layers or tender, fluffy centers (depending on your biscuit style).

It dawned on me that if you bake them close enough, they actually bake together, resulting in pull-apart biscuits! So, when strawberry season arrived, I decided to bake the biscuits together and serve them communal style. Instead of the usual individual shortcakes, I prepared the strawberries and whipped up a lemony, sweet mascarpone to top the biscuits. Guests could then help themselves, allowing me to enjoy the evening without the hassle of plating individual shortcakes.

1. Preheat the oven to 400° F. Lightly spray a 13½-by-18½-inch sheet pan with baking spray (enough for the parchment paper to adhere to the pan) and line it with parchment paper. Set aside.

2. Hull the strawberries and chop. Transfer to a medium bowl.

3. Add the brown sugar and toss with your hands or a wooden spoon to coat evenly. Cover lightly with plastic wrap and chill in the refrigerator to macerate.

4. Meanwhile, make the biscuits. In a medium bowl, whisk together the flour, salt, baking powder, and baking soda. Make a well in the center. Set aside.

5 In a small bowl, whisk together the oil, buttermilk, and sugar. Pour into the well of the flour mixture. Using your hands, fold the dry ingredients into the wet ingredients until just combined. The dough is sticky, and there will be lumps.

6 Using your hands, portion the dough into sixteen 2½- to 3-inch mounds. Place them on the prepared sheet pan ½ inch apart in 4-by-4 rows. Brush the tops with melted butter and sprinkle them with sugar in the raw.

Note: The dough will be shaggy, and the portions will be irregular, which is okay.

7 Bake for 15 to 20 minutes. or until lightly golden brown around the edges, the biscuits have risen, and the tops are slightly firm to the touch. Remove and let cool completely on a wire rack.

8 While the biscuits cool, make the whipped cream topping. In a medium bowl, use a hand mixer with the beater attachment on medium-low speed to mix together the mascarpone and powdered sugar until combined and smooth. Stop the mixer, add the lemon zest and salt, and beat on medium-low for 20 to 30 seconds until combined.

9 In a separate medium bowl, use a hand mixer with the whisk attachment on medium-low speed to whisk the heavy cream until it forms a soft peak. Gently fold the whipped cream into the mascarpone mixture until evenly combined. Chill in the refrigerator until ready to assemble.

10 To assemble, when the biscuits are completely cooled, spoon the whipped cream topping on them and smooth the layer out to cover most of them, leaving the sides exposed. Spoon strawberries over the whipped cream topping with a slotted spoon and pour some of the strawberry juices over the strawberries.

CARAMELIZED WHITE CHOCOLATE TEXAS SHEET CAKE

FOR THE CARAMELIZED WHITE CHOCOLATE

Two 12-ounce bags while chocolate chips

FOR THE CAKE

3 cups (375 g) all-purpose flour
1 tablespoon baking powder
½ teaspoon salt
½ cup (120 g) sour cream
1 cup (240 g) whole milk
1 cup (227 g) unsalted butter, softened
2 cups (400 g) granulated sugar
4 large eggs
1 tablespoon vanilla extract

FOR THE FROSTING

½ cup (113 g) unsalted butter
½ cup (120 g) heavy whipping cream
½ cup (56 g) powdered sugar
Pinch of kosher salt
Caramelized white chocolate
2½ cups (253 g) pecans, chopped

I had a conversation with my paternal grandmother that has stuck with me like a guiding star. I once asked her why my birth dad behaved the way he did and why he chose to leave. Her response was simple yet profound. She said we all face two paths in life: one that's familiar, where we repeat what we know, and another that's scarier and unknown, but offers something new. Her words resonated with me deeply and have stayed with me ever since.

Given my roots in Texas from my birth dad's side of the family, I decided to take a different direction from the classic chocolate Texas sheet cake. The cake I'm making is truly a labor of love. Caramelizing white chocolate is a slow process that requires patience, as it needs to be stirred every 10 minutes for about an hour as it bakes in the oven. But the end result is worth every minute spent, as the flavor it develops is rich and complex, making the journey of creating it well worth the unknown.

1. Prepare the caramelized white chocolate. Preheat your oven to 260° F and line a 13½-by-18½-inch sheet pan with a silicone baking mat. Spread the white chocolate chips evenly on the pan. Bake for 5 minutes.

2. After 5 minutes, with an offset spatula or the back of a wooden spoon, smooth out the melted chocolate. Bake for another 5 minutes. Smooth again.

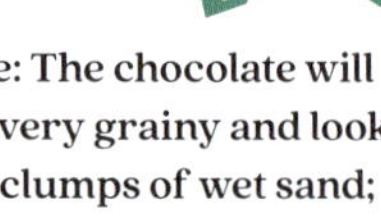

Note: The chocolate will look very grainy and look like clumps of wet sand; don't worry.

Note: The chocolate can be prepared days ahead. Store in an airtight container until ready to use.

Note: You might not use all the frosting.

3 Continue baking for another 50 minutes or until the chocolate has an even caramel color, checking every 10 minutes and stirring the chocolate to get an even caramelization.

4 Remove the pan and let cool completely on a wire rack. Once cooled, the chocolate will harden.

5 Meanwhile, prepare the cake. Increase your oven to 350° F and spray a 13½-by-18½-inch sheet pan with baking spray and line with parchment paper. Set aside.

6 In a medium bowl, whisk together the flour, baking powder, and salt. In a small bowl, whisk together the sour cream and milk. Set aside.

7 In a separate medium bowl with an electric hand mixer, cream together the butter and sugar until light and fluffy, 2 to 3 minutes. Stop the mixer and add the eggs and vanilla, and mix until combined, about 1 minute.

8 Gradually add the dry ingredients to the butter-egg mixture, alternating with the sour cream-milk mixture, until smooth and well combined.

9 Spread the batter evenly into the prepared sheet pan. Bake for 20 to 25 minutes, or until a toothpick or cake tester inserted into the center comes out clean. Cool the cake (still in the pan) completely on a wire rack.

10 Meanwhile, prepare the frosting. In a medium saucepan over medium-low heat, add the butter and heavy whipping cream, stirring occasionally with a wooden spoon until the butter is melted and the mixture is hot but not boiling.

11 Add the powdered sugar and salt, whisking vigorously until the sugar is dissolved and the mixture is smooth. Add the caramelized white chocolate and continuously stir until the chocolate is melted and the mixture is smooth. Remove from the heat and stir in the pecans.

12 Carefully pour the frosting over the cooled cake and spread evenly. Let the frosting cool completely and set before serving.

ICED LEMON SHEET CAKE

FOR THE CAKE

2 cups (250 g) all-purpose flour
1½ teaspoons baking powder
½ teaspoon baking soda
½ teaspoon kosher salt
½ cup (120 g) sour cream
½ cup (120 g) whole milk
1½ cups (300 g) granulated sugar
Zest of 2 lemons
½ cup (113 g) unsalted butter, softened
3 eggs
1 teaspoon vanilla extract
Juice of 1 lemon

FOR THE LEMON ICING

2 cups (225 g) powdered sugar
Juice and zest of 1 lemon
2 tablespoons whole milk

If I had to choose my favorite cake topping, it would be a thick, crackly icing that stays most inside. This sheet cake is bursting with zestiness! The cake-to-icing ratio is spot on, and watching the icing cascade down the sides when you slice into it is pure magic.

1. Preheat your oven to 350° F and spray a 9½-by-13½-inch quarter sheet pan with baking spray. Set aside.
2. Make the cake. In a medium bowl, whisk together the flour, baking powder, baking soda, and salt. Set aside.
3. In a small bowl, whisk together the sour cream and milk until combined. Set aside.
4. In a separate medium bowl, add the sugar and lemon zest and rub together with your fingers until evenly combined. With an electric hand mixer, cream together the lemon-sugar and butter until light and fluffy, 2 to 3 minutes. Add the eggs, vanilla, and lemon juice and mix until combined, about 1 minute.
5. Gradually add the dry ingredients to the sugar-egg mixture, alternating with the sour cream-milk mixture, until smooth and well combined.
6. Pour the batter into the prepared pan and spread evenly. Bake for 15 to 20 minutes, or until a toothpick or cake tester inserted in the middle comes out clean. Cool completely on a wire rack.
7. Meanwhile, prepare the lemon icing. In a small bowl, whisk together the powdered sugar, lemon juice, zest, and milk until smooth and evenly combined.
8. Pour the icing over the cooled cake and spread evenly. Let the icing set, about 30 minutes, before serving.

GOOEY BUTTER CORN CAKE

FOR THE CAKE

1 cup (125 g) all-purpose flour
1 cup (160 g) cornmeal
2 teaspoons baking powder
1 teaspoon baking soda
1 teaspoon kosher salt
½ cup (113 g) unsalted butter, softened
¾ cup (150 g) granulated sugar
1 egg
2 teaspoons vanilla extract
1 cup (240 g) buttermilk

FOR THE CREAM CHEESE TOPPING

One 8-ounce package cream cheese
2 cups (225 g) powdered sugar
2 eggs
1 teaspoon vanilla

If you haven't tried gooey butter cake, you're missing out on something extraordinary! It's one of those desserts where magic happens in the oven. The cake has a dense, chewy, and slightly gooey texture with a buttery base. The topping is a dreamy mix of cream cheese, sugar, and eggs, creating a creamy and indulgent layer that melts into the cake.

I first tried this cake thanks to my friend Candace from Missouri. They are just as quirky as this cake, and I love them both! Candace lives life on their own terms, and I admire their confidence. In honor of Candace's free spirit, I decided to put my own twist on the classic recipe. I used a cornmeal base, which adds an earthy sweetness to the cake. It's like cornbread living its wildest dreams. Candace approved!

1. Preheat your oven to 350° F and spray a 9½-by-13½-inch pan with baking spray and line with parchment paper, then spray the parchment. Set aside.
2. Make the cake. In a medium bowl, whisk together the flour, cornmeal, baking powder, baking soda, and salt until combined evenly.
3. In a separate medium bowl with an electric hand mixer, cream the butter and sugar until light and fluffy, 2 to 3 minutes. Stop the mixer and add the egg and vanilla; mix until combined, about 1 minute.
4. Gradually add the dry ingredients to the wet ingredients, alternating with the buttermilk until smooth and well combined.

5 Pour the batter into the prepared pan and set aside.

6 Prepare the cream cheese topping. In a medium bowl with an electric hand mixer, cream the cream cheese and powdered sugar until smooth and evenly combined, 2 to 3 minutes. Add the eggs and vanilla and mix until combined, about 1 minute.

7 Pour the topping over the cake batter and spread evenly. Bake for 25 to 30 minutes, or until a toothpick or cake tester inserted in the middle comes out clean. The cake will puff up around the cream cheese topping. Cool completely on a wire rack before serving.

DUTCH APPLE SLAB PIE

FOR THE CRUST

1⅔ cups (210 g) all-purpose flour
1 tablespoon powdered sugar
¼ teaspoon kosher salt
1 egg yolk
½ cup (113 g) unsalted butter, cold and cubed
2 to 3 tablespoons water, ice cold

FOR THE APPLE FILLING

8 cups (1,200 g) apples, peeled, cored, and sliced (6 to 8 apples)
½ cup (100 g) granulated sugar
½ cup (110 g) dark brown sugar
2 tablespoons cornstarch
2 teaspoons ground cinnamon
½ teaspoon ground nutmeg
¼ teaspoon ground ginger
½ teaspoon kosher salt

FOR THE CRUMBLE TOPPING

1 cup (125 g) all-purpose flour
½ cup (100 g) granulated sugar
½ cup (110 g) light brown sugar
½ cup (45 g) old-fashioned oats
½ teaspoon ground cinnamon
¼ teaspoon kosher salt
½ cup (113 g) unsalted butter, melted

FOR THE EGG WASH

1 egg
Splash of water

When you decide to make a slab pie, you're diving in to a process where control is a bit of a myth—and you have to be okay with that. A slab pie is like a free-spirited, open-faced pie akin to a galette or crostata. Despite your best efforts to seal the edges and fold them neatly, the dough and fruit filling will do their own thing once they're in the oven, and the filling may bubble over the edge of the crust. Embrace the fluidity and be thankful for the sheet pan's sides!

The caramelization of this Dutch apple pie creates a thick, dark sauce, and the generous crumble topping adds a delicious crunch that helps hold everything together in this delightful mess of flavors and textures. Serve warm or cold with vanilla ice cream or sweetened whipped cream.

1. Prepare the crust. Using a food processor, pulse together flour, powdered sugar, and salt until just combined. Add the egg yolk and pulse to combine.

2. Add the cubed cold butter and pulse until the mixture is coarse, like wet beach sand. Add the cold water a tablespoon at a time and pulse a few times until the mixture barely comes together. The dough will be crumbly.

3. Lay out a piece of plastic wrap on the counter long enough to wrap the dough. Dump the dough in the center of the plastic wrap. Carefully pull each side of the plastic wrap, one side at a time over the dough, making a straight clean edge (you're trying to form the dough into roughly a 6-by-6-inch square). Once covered, gently press down on the dough with your hands to compress the dough together. Use your hands to mold the sides of the dough into a square. Chill in the refrigerator for at least 1 hour or overnight.

4 Preheat your oven to 375° F. Spray a 13½-by-18½-inch sheet pan with baking spray and line with parchment paper. Set aside.

5 Prepare the apple filling. In a large bowl, add all the ingredients together and toss with your hands until the apples are evenly coated. Set aside.

6 Prepare the crumble topping. In a medium bowl, add the flour, sugars, oats, cinnamon, and salt and whisk together to combine evenly. Add the butter and with a fork, mix together to evenly combine and make a crumble texture. Set aside.

7 Remove the dough from the refrigerator and dust a clean surface with flour. With a floured rolling pin, gently roll the dough out a ¼ inch thick. Don't worry if the dough cracks, you can use leftover dough to fill in the cracks. Transfer the dough to the prepared pan, making sure it's centered in the pan and the overhang dough is even around the edges as much as possible. Edges will be jagged and that is okay; slab pies are rustic in nature.

8 Pour the apple filling over the crust and spread into an even, heaping layer. Evenly scatter the crumble topping over the apples, making sure to cover all four edges where the apples meet the pie dough.

9 There are two options for forming the pie edges: 1) roll the edges onto itself, forming a border around the pie for a more uniform look, or 2) fold the overhang edges over the top of the pie for a more rustic look, similar to a galette or crostata. I prefer option 2 for apple pies.

10 Make the egg wash. In a small bowl, add the egg and a splash of water and whisk together vigorously until evenly combined. Using a pastry brush, brush the pie edges with the egg wash. Bake for 50 to 60 minutes, or until the crust is dark golden brown and the apple filling is bubbling. Cool on a wire rack for 30 minutes before serving. Serve warm or cold .

APRICOT SLAB PIE

FOR THE CRUST

1⅔ cups (210 g) all-purpose flour
1 tablespoon powdered sugar
¼ teaspoon kosher salt
1 egg yolk
½ cup (113 g) unsalted butter, cold and cubed
2 to 3 tablespoons water, ice cold

FOR THE FILLING

2 cups (480 g) boiling water
3 cups (550 g) dried apricots
½ cup (100 g) granulated sugar
¼ cup (55 g) light brown sugar
2 tablespoons cornstarch
1 teaspoon vanilla extract
½ teaspoon ground cinnamon
¼ teaspoon ground ginger
¼ teaspoon kosher salt
½ cup (35 g) sliced almonds
½ cup (160 g) apricot preserves

FOR THE FRANGIPANE

¼ cup (56 g) unsalted butter, softened
½ cup (100 g) granulated sugar
2 eggs
1 teaspoon almond extract
1 cup (96 g) almond flour
Powdered sugar for garnish

FOR THE EGG WASH

1 egg
Splash of water

Despite living in the desert, my grandparents managed to create a lush garden oasis. Their front yard was a sea of thick green grass and trees wrapped with ivy. They had a beautiful rose garden in the backyard, a vibrant vegetable patch, and a mini orchard with pear, apple, and apricot trees. However, between 1987 and 1992, California endured one of its worst droughts, and gradually their lush oasis dried up.

During those years that it thrived, I found solace in their garden oasis, escaping reality and immersing myself in a world where I could be Justin, without any constraints or societal expectations. This apricot slab pie is a tribute to that carefree version of myself, a reminder of a time when I could daydream without the weight of the world on my shoulders.

Since fresh apricots can be hard to come by, in this recipe I rehydrated dried apricots and chopped them up to scatter over a base layer of frangipane in the pie. Just before the pie is done baking, I sprinkle sliced almonds on top. Once it's slightly cooled, I brush apricot preserves over the surface to seal in all the flavors and give the pie a glossy finish.

Part pie, part tart, this bake embodies the essence of freedom and whimsy, a nod to a time when life was simpler, and dreams were limitless.

1. Prepare the crust. Using a food processor, pulse together the flour, powdered sugar, and salt until just combined. Add the egg yolk and pulse to combine.
2. Add the cubed cold butter and pulse until the mixture is coarse, like wet beach sand. Add the cold water a tablespoon at a time and pulse a few times until the mixture barely comes together. The dough will be crumbly.

3 Lay out a piece of plastic wrap on the counter long enough to wrap the dough. Dump the dough in the center of the plastic wrap. Carefully pull each side of the plastic wrap, one side at a time over the dough, making a straight clean edge (you're trying to form the dough into roughly a 6-by-6-inch square). Once covered, gently press down on the dough with your hands to compress the dough together. Use your hands to mold the sides of the dough into a square. Chill in the refrigerator for at least 1 hour or overnight.

4 Preheat your oven to 375°F. Spray a 13½-by-18½-inch sheet pan with baking spray and line with parchment paper. Set aside.

5 Prepare the apricot filling. In a medium saucepan over high heat, add the water and bring to a boil. Turn off the heat and add the apricots, ensuring all are submerged. Cover the pan and let them rehydrate for 30 minutes. Drain and dry.

6 Chop the apricots and place in a medium bowl. Add the sugars, cornstarch, vanilla, cinnamon, ginger, and salt. Stir with a wooden spoon until evenly combined and the apricots are coated; the mixture will be thick. Set aside.

7 Prepare the frangipane. In a separate medium bowl with an electric hand mixer, cream the butter and sugar until light and fluffy, 2 to 3 minutes. Add the eggs and almond extract and mix until combined, about 1 minute. Add the almond flour and mix until just combined. Set aside.

8 Remove the dough from the refrigerator and dust a clean surface with flour. With a floured rolling pin, gently roll the dough out a ¼ inch thick. Don't worry if the dough cracks; you can use leftover dough to fill in the cracks. Transfer the dough to the prepared pan, making sure it's centered on the pan and the overhang dough is even around the edges as much as possible. The edges will be jagged and that is okay; slab pies are rustic in nature.

9 Spread the frangipane in an even layer over the pie dough. Pour the apricot mixture over the frangipane and spread evenly.

10 There are two options for forming the pie edges: 1) roll the edges onto itself, forming a border around the pie for a more uniform look, or 2) fold the overhang edges over the top of the pie for a more rustic look, similar to a galette or crostata. I prefer option 1 for this pie.

11 Make the egg wash. In a small bowl, add the egg and a splash of water and whisk together vigorously until evenly combined. Using a pastry brush, brush the pie edges with the egg wash. Bake for 30 minutes. Remove the pie and sprinkle almonds over the top; return to the oven and continue baking for another 10 to 15 minutes, or until the crust is dark golden brown and the frangipane is puffed up.

12 Cool on a wire rack for 10 minutes. Meanwhile, in a heat-proof bowl, add the apricot preserves and microwave for 10 to 15 seconds, just enough to loosen the preserves. With a pastry brush, brush the apricot-almond layer with the preserves. Do not brush the pie crust. Continue letting cool. Serve warm or cold, dusted with the powdered sugar.

Cherish these moments.

Slab pies are unruly—embrace the chaos! Trust that getting the perfect shape isn't the point; it's all about the deliciousness inside.

Clockwise from left: Saucepan Brownies (page 29), Oatmeal Butterscotch Cookie Bars (page 97), Scotcheroos (page 73), C. B.'s Date Nut Bread (page 131), and Apricot Slab Pie (page 121)

PRIDE CELEBRATION SLAB TART

I'm not big on literal rainbow representations, preferring to let queer excellence shine in other ways. But I enjoy a bit of satire, and if berries can be arranged as the nation's flag on the tops of desserts, then why not the pride flag? In true queer fashion, this slab tart is a bit extra, featuring a buttery, salty shortbread crust, a creamy filling infused with vanilla bean, cream cheese, and mascarpone, all topped with an assortment of fruits in a rainbow pattern.

FOR THE CRUST

1 cup (227 g) unsalted butter, room temperature

½ cup (100 g) granulated sugar

2 cups (250 g) all-purpose flour

¼ teaspoon kosher salt

FOR THE CREAM CHEESE FILLING

Two 8-ounce packages cream cheese

One 8-ounce package mascarpone

1½ cups (170 g) powdered sugar

¼ cup (60 g) heavy whipping cream

1 teaspoon vanilla bean paste

FOR THE FRUIT TOPPING

½ pint raspberries

One 15-ounce can mandarin oranges, drained

One 20-ounce can pineapple slices, drained and halved

3 kiwis, peeled and sliced

½ pint blueberries

½ pint blackberries

½ cup (160 g) apricot preserves

1. Preheat your oven to 350° F and spray a 9½-by-13½-inch sheet pan and line with parchment paper. Set aside.
2. Prepare the crust. In a medium bowl with an electric hand mixer, cream together the butter and sugar until light and fluffy, 2 to 3 minutes. Add the flour and salt and mix until crumbly.
3. Press the mixture into the bottom of the prepared pan to form an even layer. Bake the crust for 20 to 25 minutes, or until golden brown. Cool completely on a wire rack.
4. Meanwhile, prepare the cream cheese filling. In a medium bowl with an electric hand mixer, cream together the cream cheese, mascarpone, and powdered sugar until creamy and smooth, 2 to 3 minutes. Add the heavy whipping cream and vanilla bean paste and mix until smooth and evenly combined. Set aside.
5. Once the crust is cooled, pour the cream cheese mixture over the crust and spread evenly. Arrange the fruit in 2-inch-wide columns over the cream cheese layer starting from left to right: raspberries (red), mandarin oranges (orange), pineapple (yellow), kiwi (green), blueberries (blue), and blackberries (purple).

Note: Since fruit can vary in size, you might not use all the fruit suggested.

A rainbow shirt isn't necessary for serving, but it definitely adds a nice touch.

6. In a heatproof bowl, add the apricot preserves and microwave for 10 to 15 seconds, just enough to loosen the preserves. With a pastry brush, brush the fruit layer with the preserves. Chill in the refrigerator until ready to serve.

CHAPTER THREE

LOAF PANS

Let's celebrate the humble loaf pans. With their simple design and durable build, these unassuming pans have been the vessel for many of my most treasured family recipes. I wouldn't call them easy, but I also wouldn't label them as innovative; I would say they are reliably straightforward.

Loaf pans are often seen as homey, perhaps even old-fashioned. If that's the case, consider me an old soul because I adore them. Knowing the boundaries of what these pans can achieve provides a sense of comfort in the kitchen. They're perfect for quick breads, loaves, small cakes, icebox cakes, and no-bake desserts. Your creativity is contained, not limited, just simply focused.

In my upbringing, quick breads were the go-to for casual gatherings or visiting a friend's home for some face-to-face catch-up time. You'd bake it fresh in the morning, let it cool, wrap it in parchment and baker's twine, and deliver this sweet treat to be shared over coffee or tea (perhaps even wine). To me, they symbolize baking with love.

Loaf pans remind me of my time in Boston. As a group of twentysomethings, our chosen family was resourceful in affording city living and creating bonds reminiscent of family ties. Occasionally, a quick bread would appear, or during our time together in one of our apartments, we'd find ourselves in the kitchen whipping up something delicious with limited resources. But, whether it was a loaf cake, quick bread, or an icebox cake on a hot Boston summer day, we always felt rich and fulfilled.

The loaf pan was always there, a symbol of our reliance on each other, ready and waiting for when we needed it.

C. B.'S DATE NUT BREAD

2 cups (480 g) water
3 cups (450 g) dates, chopped
2 cups (250 g) all-purpose flour
1 cup (220 g) light brown sugar
1 teaspoon kosher salt
1 teaspoon baking powder
½ teaspoon baking soda
¼ teaspoon ground cinnamon
¼ teaspoon ground nutmeg
2 eggs
½ cup (120 g) buttermilk
1 cup (198 g) vegetable oil
1 teaspoon vanilla extract
1 cup (105 g) walnuts, chopped

Why don't we hear about date nut bread more? Sure, dates might not be the trendiest ingredient, but classics are classics for a reason. If old-fashioned trends can make a comeback, why not this bread? This recipe is my attempt to re-create my grandmother C. B.'s version, which I had to do completely by memory as I don't have her recipe. I start by soaking the dates to make them tender, not chewy. Soaking also helps them meld into the bread, giving it that extra moistness, and to spread the date flavor throughout. You can skip the walnuts if they're not your thing, but their crunch adds a nice touch. In true honor of C. B., serve warm with a generous smear of salted butter.

1. Spray a 9-by-5-inch loaf pan with baking spray and line with parchment paper, leaving an overhang along the long edges. Spray the parchment. Set aside.

2. In a medium saucepan over high heat, add the water and bring to a boil. Turn off the heat and add the dates, ensuring that all are submerged. Cover the pan and let them rehydrate for 30 minutes. Drain and dry.

3. In a medium bowl, whisk together the flour, sugar, salt, baking powder, baking soda, cinnamon, and nutmeg until evenly combined. Make a well in the center.

4. In a small bowl, whisk together the eggs, buttermilk, oil, and vanilla until evenly combined. Pour the mixture into the center of the well. With a rubber spatula or wooden spoon, gently fold the ingredients together until just combined. Fold in the dates and walnuts.

5 Pour the batter into the prepared pan, tap the pan to release air bubbles, and level the batter. Place in a cold oven and set the temperature to 325°F. Bake for 70 to 80 minutes, or until a toothpick or cake tester inserted in the middle comes out clean. Cool on a wire rack in the pan for 10 minutes, then remove from the pan using the parchment overhang and continue cooling on the rack.

BAKING TIP: COLD OVEN BAKING WORKS WONDERS

Cold oven baking is a technique that can enhance the texture and flavor of various baked goods, including quick breads and cookies. By placing them in a cold oven and then turning it on, you allow them to heat up along with the oven gradually. For some bakes, this slower start can lead to more even baking, improved rise, and a tender, moist crumb.

For quick bread, starting in a cold oven can help promote a more even rise and prevent over-browning on the top. The gentle heat at the beginning allows the leavening agents to work their magic without the risk of burning the exterior.

Similarly, beginning cookies in a cold oven can result in a more controlled spread, leading to thicker, chewier cookies. The gradual heat also gives flavors more time to develop, enhancing the overall taste.

Remember to adjust your baking times accordingly when using cold ovens, as they'll take longer to bake.

STRAWBERRY-ZUCCHINI QUICK BREAD

- 3 cups (420 g) grated zucchini (2 to 3 medium zucchini; see step 2)
- 2 cups (250 g) all-purpose flour
- 1 cup (220 g) light brown sugar
- 1 teaspoon kosher salt
- 1 teaspoon baking powder
- ½ teaspoon baking soda
- 1 teaspoon ground cinnamon
- ¼ teaspoon ground nutmeg
- ¼ teaspoon ground ginger
- ¼ teaspoon ground clove
- 2 eggs
- ½ cup (120 g) buttermilk
- 1 cup (198 g) vegetable oil
- 1 teaspoon vanilla extract
- ¼ cup (85 g) strawberry preserves

I'm a huge fan of flavor combos that make people do a double take. Whenever I bring out this quick bread, I love seeing the looks of surprise and confusion—like, "Did they really just put that together?" But the truth is, I've been enjoying zucchini quick bread with strawberry preserves for as long as I can remember.

The fresh, bright flavors of the zucchini and strawberry, and the subtle, cozy warmth from the spices create a vibe perfect for spring and summer baking. And you know what's even better? When the skeptics give it a try and end up loving it. I get to enjoy a little victory dance in my head and say, "See, I told you it's delicious!"

1. Spray a 9-by-5-inch loaf pan with baking spray and line with parchment paper, leaving an overhang along the long edges. Spray the parchment. Set aside.

2. Using a box grater, grate the zucchini on the side with the biggest holes. Place the shredded zucchini in a colander, lay a few paper towels over the zucchini and press firmly to drain the excess liquid. Set aside.

3. In a medium bowl, whisk together the flour, sugar, salt, baking powder, baking soda, cinnamon, nutmeg, ginger, and clove until evenly combined. Make a well in the center.

4. In a small bowl, whisk together the eggs, buttermilk, oil, and vanilla until evenly combined. Pour the mixture into the center of the well. With a rubber spatula or wooden spoon, gently fold the ingredients together until just combined. Fold in the zucchini.

continues

5 Pour the batter into the prepared pan, tap the pan to release air bubbles, and level the batter. Dollop strawberry preserves down the center of the batter and with a butter knife, gently swirl into the batter from left to right in a zig-zag pattern, making sure not to push into the batter too deep. If pushed too far down before baking, the preserves will sink to the bottom of the pan.

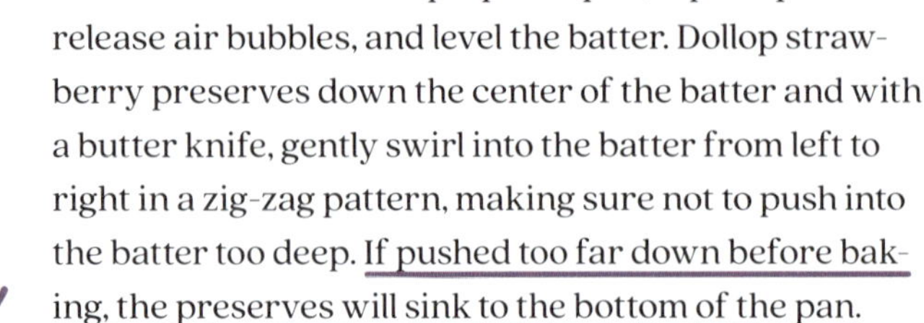

Note: You want the preserves to stay as close to the top as possible; as the bread bakes, the preserves will sink.

6 Place into a cold oven and set the temperature to 350°F. Bake for 55 to 65 minutes, or until a toothpick or cake tester inserted in the middle comes out clean. Cool on a wire rack in the pan for 10 minutes, then remove from the pan, lifting the parchment overhang and continue cooling.

BAKING TIP: SIZE DOES MATTER

Size can make a big difference when baking in a loaf pan. If a recipe doesn't specify the size of the loaf pan, it can leave you wondering which one to use. That's where the two-thirds rule comes in handy: Fill the pan only two-thirds of the way to prevent any potential spillage.

But why aren't loaf pan sizes regularly indicated in recipes? It's a bit of a historical mystery. Back in the day (we're talking a long time ago), loaf pans were typically 9-by-5 inches, so there was no need to specify the size. However, nowadays, loaf pans come in all sizes, and what's considered a standard size can vary from brand to brand.

To save yourself the stress of guessing, just remember the two-thirds rule. It's a simple way to ensure your loaf bakes up perfectly every time, regardless of the size of your pan. If you have a good amount of leftover batter, you can portion the remaining batter into lined muffin pans and bake for 15 to 25 minutes, or until golden brown and a toothpick inserted in the middle comes out clean.

GRAPEFRUIT POPPY SEED QUICK BREAD

FOR THE BREAD

1 cup (200 g) granulated sugar
2 tablespoons grapefruit zest
2 cups (250 g) all-purpose flour
1 teaspoon baking powder
½ teaspoon baking soda
1 teaspoon kosher salt
2 tablespoons poppy seeds
2 eggs
½ cup (120 g) buttermilk
1 cup (198 g) vegetable oil
¼ cup (60 g) grapefruit juice
1 teaspoon vanilla extract

FOR THE ICING

¼ cup (30 g) powdered sugar
¼ cup (60 g) grapefruit juice
2 tablespoons unsalted butter, melted

As a kid, I was obsessed with lemon poppy seed bread. But it had to be Mrs. Whittaker's version, my third-grade teacher. Her loaf was this beautiful golden color, packed with poppy seeds, and had just the right balance of sweet and tart. The absolute best part, though, was the crackled icing that covered all four sides of the loaf.

The signature crater in the middle of the bread was where the icing would pool, and those two or three bites from underneath were my absolute favorite. The icing would soak into the crumb, making it extra moist and sticky—pure joy for a kid like me.

My take on this classic uses a different citrus, but I stick to Mrs. Whittaker's cues for the bread itself. While I don't ice all four sides as she did, I do pour the icing over the loaf while it's still in the pan right out of the oven. This allows the icing to soak into the bread and pool in several spots, giving more of those favorite bites throughout.

1 Spray a 9-by-5-inch loaf pan with baking spray and line with parchment paper, leaving an overhang along the long edges. Spray the parchment. Set aside.

2 Make the bread. In a small bowl, add the sugar and zest. With your fingers, rub the sugar and zest together until evenly combined.

3 In a medium bowl, whisk together the flour, sugar-zest, baking powder, baking soda, salt, and poppy seeds until evenly combined. Make a well in the center.

4. In a small bowl, whisk together the eggs, buttermilk, oil, grapefruit juice, and vanilla until evenly combined. Pour the mixture into the center of the well. With a rubber spatula or wooden spoon, gently fold the ingredients together until just combined.
5. Pour the batter into the prepared pan, tap the pan to release air bubbles, and level the batter. Place in the cold oven and set the temperature to 325°F. Bake for 50 to 60 minutes, or until a toothpick or cake tester inserted in the middle comes out clean. Place on a wire rack and let cool.
6. Meanwhile, prepare the icing. In a small bowl, whisk together the powdered sugar, grapefruit juice, and butter until evenly combined and smooth. Poor the icing over the warm bread. Continue cooling and let the icing set before serving.

PEACH COBBLER BREAD

FOR THE BREAD

1¼ cups (282 g) unsalted butter
1 pound frozen peaches, thawed, drained, and dried (see step 3)
2 cups (250 g) all-purpose flour
1 cup (220 g) light brown sugar
1 teaspoon baking powder
½ teaspoon baking soda
1½ teaspoons ground cinnamon
½ teaspoon ground ginger
½ teaspoon ground cardamom
1 teaspoon kosher salt
2 eggs
½ cup (120 g) buttermilk
1 teaspoon vanilla extract

FOR THE CRUMBLE

⅓ cup (73 g) light brown sugar
⅓ cup plus 2 tablespoons (72 g) all-purpose flour
Pinch of kosher salt
¼ cup (57 g) unsalted butter, browned

This recipe combines some of my favorite things: peaches, quick bread, cobbler, and brown butter. I've always loved the way peaches flavor baked goods, creating pockets of delicate goodness with bursts of stone fruit freshness.

In this recipe, I use brown butter to bridge the gap between the fresh fruit's acidity and the warm, earthy spices. The brown butter subtly infuses into the bread, adding a hidden depth; while in the crumble, it gives a delightful little pop here and there.

1. Preheat your oven to 325°F. Spray a 9-by-5-inch loaf pan with baking spray and line with parchment paper, leaving an overhang along the long edges; spray the parchment. Set aside.

2. Make the bread. In a medium saucepan over medium heat, add the butter. Melt the butter, swirling the pan occasionally to evenly distribute the browning and to prevent the butter from browning too quickly. Once melted, the butter will begin to foam up; at this point, lower the heat to medium-low and continue to brown, occasionally swirling the pan. The crackling will start to lower, and the foam will decrease. At this point, watch the center of the foam; once the center begins to turn a golden, nutty color, swirl the pan evenly and, once evenly golden, remove the pan from heat. Pour the brown butter into a small heatproof bowl through a fine mesh sieve. Set aside and let cool.

3. Meanwhile, with a paper towel, pat down the thawed and drained frozen peaches, making sure to remove excess moisture. Roughly chop the peaches and set aside.

4 In a medium bowl, whisk together the flour, sugar, baking powder, baking soda, cinnamon, ginger, cardamom, and salt until evenly combined. Make a well in the center.

5 In a small bowl, whisk together the eggs, buttermilk, 1 cup (227 g) of the brown butter, and vanilla until evenly combined. Pour the mixture into the center of the well. With a rubber spatula or wooden spoon, gently fold the ingredients together until just combined. Fold in the peaches.

6 Pour the batter into the prepared pan, tap the pan to release air bubbles, and level the batter. Set aside.

7 Prepare the crumble. In a medium bowl, whisk together the brown sugar, flour, and salt until well combined. Add the remaining brown butter and with a fork, mix together until evenly combined and crumbles form. Evenly scatter crumble over batter.

8 Bake for 55 to 65 minutes, or until a toothpick or cake tester inserted in the middle comes out clean. Place on a wire rack and let cool.

BAKING TIP:
THAW, DRAIN, AND DRY FROZEN FRUIT BEFORE ADDING TO BATTER

Frozen fruit is convenient, especially when baking with a fruit that is not in season. But, when the fruit is frozen, excess water develops. If not removed before adding to the batter, it can compromise the final bake. Before doing anything in a recipe that calls for frozen fruit, my first step is prepping the fruit. The process is simple: thaw, drain, and pat dry with a paper towel. It's a little bit of prep work that will make a huge difference in your final product.

This is a best practice because it:

AVOIDS EXCESS MOISTURE: Frozen fruit contains excess water; if you toss it straight into your batter, all that extra moisture can make your baked goods soggy. Thawing the fruit first removes the water, which helps to keep the texture of the bake just right.

ENSURES EVEN BAKING: Adding frozen fruit to the batter can decrease its temperature, leading to uneven baking. Thawing the fruit to room temperature helps everything bake evenly, so you don't end up with undercooked or overcooked spots.

KEEPS THE FRUIT INTACT: Thawing and gently patting the fruit dry helps maintain its shape and texture. This way, the fruit doesn't turn into mush and ruin the look and feel of your baked goods.

BOOSTS THE FLAVOR: Extra water from the frozen fruit can dilute the flavors in your batter. Removing that water keeps the fruit's natural flavors concentrated, making your baked goods taste even better.

JASPER'S "TASTES LIKE COOKIE DOUGH" FUDGE

- 4 cups (480 g) graham cracker crumbs
- ½ teaspoon kosher salt
- 2 cups (200 g) mini marshmallows
- ½ cup (70 g) salted peanuts, chopped
- 1 cup (170 g) mini semi-sweet chocolate chips
- 1 cup (80 g) sweetened shredded coconut, toasted
- Two 11.6-ounce cans sweetened condensed coconut milk

Kids are amazing, especially when they're in the kitchen. Their creativity knows no bounds, and they're capable of coming up with some truly imaginative dishes. When I was working on this cookbook, my son, Jasper, was right there with me, soaking it all in and exploring his own culinary creativity. Early on, when I hit a writer's block, I turned to Jasper for inspiration. I let him make whatever he wanted, and this fudge recipe is one of his creations, with a little guidance from me on how to bring it to life. The ingredients might sound unusual, but that's the beauty of a kid's imagination. And true to its name, this fudge really does taste like cookie dough, a testament to Jasper's inventive spirit in the kitchen.

1. Spray a 9-by-5-inch loaf pan with baking spray and line with parchment paper, leaving an overhang along the long edges. Spray the parchment. Set aside.
2. In a medium bowl, whisk together the graham cracker crumbs and salt. Fold in the marshmallows, peanuts, chocolate chips, and shredded coconut until evenly combined. Fold in the condensed coconut milk until evenly combined and the mixture is thick.
3. Pour the mixture into the prepared pan and press firmly to compact into the pan in an even layer. Cover in plastic wrap and chill in the refrigerator for at least 2 hours, overnight preferred.
4. Once set, remove the fudge from the pan, pulling up from the overhang of the parchment paper. With a sharp knife, slice the fudge in 1- to 1½-inch-thick slices. Then cut each slice into 6 even squares. Store in an airtight container and chill in the refrigerator until ready to serve.

CHOCOLATE CHERRY SODA CAKE

FOR THE CAKE

1½ cups (187 g) all-purpose flour
½ cup (42 g) cocoa powder
1 teaspoon baking powder
½ teaspoon baking soda
½ teaspoon kosher salt
½ cup (120 g) buttermilk
½ cup (112 g) cherry soda
½ cup (113 g) unsalted butter, softened
1 cup (200 g) granulated sugar
2 eggs
1 teaspoon vanilla extract
½ cup (100 g) maraschino cherries, drained (liquid reserved), and chopped

FOR THE MARASCHINO BUTTERCREAM

½ cup (113 g) unsalted butter, softened
⅔ cup (80 g) powdered sugar
Pinch of kosher salt
4 teaspoons reserved maraschino liquid
Dark chocolate bar for garnish
Maraschino cherries for garnish

This recipe perfectly exemplifies how different life moments can blend into a single, inspiring recipe. I grew up along Route 66, where a nearby '50s diner served fountain sodas with customizable syrups like chocolate and cherry, reminiscent of old-fashioned soda shops.

My hometown had a Harvey House, a series of hotels with top-notch restaurants along the railroad in the late 19th and early 20th centuries, and considered to be the first chain in America. My great-grandmother was among the first "Harvey girls," the employees of the restaurant. As a child, I vividly recall discovering a menu from Harvey House featuring a chocolate and maraschino cherry loaf cake. That memory stayed with me through the years.

It wasn't until I was 31, at a funeral, that I tried my first soda cake—boxed cake mix baked with any type of soda that complemented the cake mix as the sole added ingredient. It was a lightbulb moment where these three distinct memories converged, inspiring the creation of this cake.

If you enjoy the flavors of cherry soda, chocolate, and maraschino cherries, you'll adore this cake. It's moist, chocolaty, not overly sweet, and topped with a delightful maraschino pink buttercream for that retro touch.

1 Preheat your oven to 350°F and spray a 9-by-5-inch loaf pan with baking spray and line with parchment paper, leaving an overhang along the long edges, spray parchment. Set aside.

2 In a medium bowl, whisk together the flour, cocoa powder, baking powder, baking soda, and salt until evenly combined. Set aside.

continues

3. In a small bowl, whisk together the buttermilk and cherry soda. Set aside.
4. In a separate medium bowl with an electric hand mixer, cream the butter and sugar until light and fluffy, 2 to 3 minutes. Add the eggs and vanilla and mix until combined, about 1 minute.
5. Gradually add the dry ingredients to the butter-sugar ingredients, alternating with the buttermilk-soda mixture until smooth and well combined. Fold in the cherries.
6. Pour the batter into the prepared pan, tap the pan to release the air bubbles, and level the batter. Bake for 40 to 50 minutes, or until a toothpick or cake tester inserted in the middle comes out clean. Set on a wire rack and let cool completely.
7. Meanwhile, prepare the buttercream. In a medium bowl with an electric hand mixer, cream the butter, powdered sugar, and salt until light and fluffy, 2 to 3 minutes. Add the maraschino liquid and mix until evenly combined and pale pink.
8. Once the cake is cooled, remove from the pan lifting up from the parchment overhang. Frost the top of the cake with buttercream in an even layer. With a fine grater, generously shave the chocolate bar over the buttercream. Top with maraschino cherries.

HONEY-ALMOND FINANCIER LOAF

FOR THE FINANCIER

½ cup (113 g) unsalted butter
½ cup (48 g) almond flour
½ cup (62 g) all-purpose flour
½ cup (100 g) granulated sugar
4 egg whites
½ teaspoon almond extract
Pinch of kosher salt
¼ cup (85 g) honey
Sliced almonds for topping (optional)

FOR THE GLAZE

¼ cup (85 g) honey
1 tablespoon water
Powdered sugar for garnish (optional)

You wouldn't normally associate financiers with potlucks, but they hold a special place in my heart thanks to an experience and friendships that changed my life. Financiers are these delightful French almond cakes—light, moist, and bursting with flavor—perfect for enjoying with tea or coffee.

When I was first diving in to pastry as a career, I became friends with two chefs who worked downstairs from my apartment, Kristen and Stephanie. Our friendship blossomed naturally; we shared similar interests and just got along well. Plus, they couldn't resist my two English cream golden retriever puppies. During one chat, I asked Kristen for an easy French pastry recipe to try. She recommended financiers and even lent me a cookbook. I must have baked dozens of them, practicing until I perfected the recipe on my own.

Kristen and Stephanie opened up their world to me, and it kickstarted my professional journey. While we've all gone our separate ways now, I keep them close to my heart. They remind me how friendships, even with strangers at first, can push us to aspire to new heights.

So here's my tribute to Kristen and Stephanie: a big honey financier loaf to share. It's a reminder to stay open to new experiences and friendships, and to enjoy the journey wherever it takes you.

1 Preheat your oven to 350° F and spray a 9-by-5-inch loaf pan with baking spray and line with parchment paper, leaving an overhang along the long edges. Set aside.

continues →

2 Make the financier. In a medium saucepan over medium heat, add the butter. Melt the butter, swirling the pan occasionally to evenly distribute the browning and to prevent the butter from burning too quickly. Once melted, the butter will begin to foam up; at this point, lower the heat to medium-low and continue to brown, occasionally swirling the pan. The crackling will start to lower, and the foam will decrease; at this point, watch the center of the foam. Once the center begins to turn a golden, nutty color, swirl the pan evenly and, once evenly golden, remove the pan from the heat. Pour the brown butter into a small heatproof bowl through a fine mesh sieve. Set aside and let cool.

3 In a medium bowl, whisk together the almond flour, flour, and granulated sugar.

4 In a separate medium bowl with an electric hand mixer, beat the egg whites until frothy but not stiff. With a rubber spatula or wooden spoon, gradually fold in the flour mixture until just combined.

5 Add the almond extract, salt, honey, and the browned butter to the batter, stirring gently until smooth.

6 Pour the batter into the prepared pan, smoothing the top with a spatula. Sprinkle sliced almonds over the top. Bake for 25 to 30 minutes, or until the cake is golden brown and a toothpick or cake tester inserted in the middle comes out clean.

7 Remove the cake from the oven and let it cool in the pan for 10 minutes.

8 Meanwhile, prepare the honey glaze. In a small heatproof bowl, add the honey and water and heat in a microwave for 10 to 25 seconds. Whisk vigorously and pour over the warm financier.

9 Using the parchment paper overhang, lift the cake out of the pan and transfer it to a wire rack, pull down the sides of the parchment paper, and let the honey glaze run down the side. Continue to cool completely.

10 Once cooled, dust with powdered sugar, if desired.

Chocolate Cherry Soda Cake (page 145)

From left: Cranberry-Orange Fluff Salad (page 251), Boozy Coconut Rum Bundt Cake (page 222), Chocolate Cherry Soda Cake (page 145)

KNOWING WHEN TO

I LIVED in Boston for almost 13 years, with the last three in a cozy 750-square-foot apartment overlooking Tremont Street in the city's art district. It was wrapped in ivy that swept across the bay windows, and the cityscape glimmered in the winter during night snowfalls. The apartment was directly above a restaurant, so the patio chatter echoed into my bedroom, creating a vibrant atmosphere that I loved.

Boston holds a special place in my heart. It's where I experienced life independently, living far away from my family for 13 years. Among my large group of friends, about 15 of us were inseparable, operating as each other's family. Leaving was difficult because so many memories were made in that space. The concept of a chosen family is often linked to individuals who collectively foster a nucleus family outside of blood ties. But, unlike previous experiences, I settled into my environment, convinced I would live in Boston for the rest of my life. I made a home and connected the pieces together to make the city the environment I had desired my entire life, a place to call home that felt like home.

As a community, LGBTQIA+ individuals are seeking not only the people but also the place to establish a family. When we think of family, a physical environment is part of the equation, where we feel safe, seen, and respected to live freely and to host our transformation into no longer hiding. I found all of that with Boston, so leaving was difficult because I knew I was uprooting my life and was afraid I wouldn't find it again.

I connected with Boston so closely that I often call it home despite being a California native. I never look forward to returning to California, but I get giddy when an upcoming trip to Beantown is approaching. It's fair to say Boston is my chosen family home, whereas California is my blood family home. Between the two, I favor Boston,

SAY GOODBYE

as it defines me much better than where I grew up. I embody the Boston spirit; despite its many flaws, it's where I took inventory of the characteristics and behaviors I loved and set aside those I disagreed with, connecting the pieces to discover myself more authentically.

I lived in many apartments for those 13 years, but my last one is what I think of when I think back to home: the off-white walls, the tiny kitchen, and the three-floor walk up. My backyard was the cherished park down the street, and the neighbors embodied neighborly kindness.

When I finally had my life of over a decade packed and the car loaded, I watched the cityscape get smaller in the distance as I drove away and started crying, thinking, *Am I making the right decision?* I was leaving everything behind with nothing planned ahead; I just uprooted my life for the unexpected that was waiting in North Carolina. I reached for a car snack a friend had packed, grabbing the banana-nut quick bread as I said goodbye to home.

White Wine

POTLUCK'S COMPANION, ICE CREAM

Potluck desserts and vanilla ice cream are a match. Many recipes in this cookbook suggest pairing them with vanilla or buttermilk ice cream, and for good reason. While grabbing a pint or two from the store is convenient, if you have the chance to whip up your own at home, I highly recommend it. And guess what? You don't even need an ice cream maker for it. I'm a big fan of the no-churn method, which means you can make ice cream whenever the craving strikes, especially if you have a loaf pan on hand.

The following two recipes are flavors that complement any dessert in this book: buttermilk and sweet cream. If you haven't tried buttermilk ice cream before, you're in for a treat. It pairs beautifully with fruit-based desserts and anything with warm spices or rich caramel flavors.

NO-CHURN BUTTERMILK ICE CREAM

2 cups (480 g) heavy whipping cream
One 14-ounce can sweetened condensed milk
½ cup (120 g) buttermilk
1 teaspoon vanilla extract

1 In a medium bowl with an electric hand mixer, whip the heavy cream until stiff peaks form.

2 In a separate medium bowl, whisk together the sweetened condensed milk, buttermilk, and vanilla extract. Fold the whipped cream into the condensed milk mixture until evenly combined.

3 Pour the mixture into a 9-by-5-inch loaf pan and smooth the top. Cover with plastic wrap and freeze for at least 6 hours or until firm.

NO-CHURN SWEET CREAM ICE CREAM

2 cups (480 g) heavy whipping cream

One 14-ounce can sweetened condensed milk

1 teaspoon vanilla bean paste

1. In a medium bowl with an electric hand mixer, whip the heavy cream until stiff peaks form.
2. In a separate medium bowl, whisk together the sweetened condensed milk and vanilla bean paste. Fold the whipped cream into the condensed milk mixture until evenly combined.
3. Pour the mixture into a 9-by-5-inch loaf pan and smooth the top. Cover with plastic wrap and freeze for at least 6 hours or until firm.

polaroid

SUMMER IN P-TOWN: ICEBOX CAKES

Summer has always been a season of transformation for me. Not every summer, but since my 20s, I've come to anticipate change when the warmer weather arrives. It all started when I was 22. I was spending a lot of time in Provincetown (P-Town), Massachusetts, for work, and it was my first experience in an environment that was constantly open and accepting of being gay. My anxiety melted away, and I carried myself with a newfound confidence. There was no lingering fear that something bad might happen or that someone would react negatively. It was a queer utopia, and I was reveling in every moment.

Those two and a half months were filled with queer joy, like something out of a queer rom-com. I was in P-Town several days a week, so my job had a designated house for us to stay in. I shared the house with five other people from my organization and five more from another group working on the Cape that summer. The 10 of us became fast friends, and every evening after work, we'd either explore Commercial Street or stay in, avoiding the tourists, and enjoy dinner together at home. That summer changed my mindset. It made me realize that I could live happily and have a life that felt safe and welcoming. I cherish that time of youth, being fully aware that my perspective was evolving and that good things were possible.

On our last night together before the end of the summer, we had a grand dinner on the back porch. The owner of the house hired a chef, and we ate fresh seafood caught that morning, sipped on margaritas, and danced freely to early 2000s bangers. The final dish we shared was a cranberry bog icebox cake: layers of cold, sweet cream and graham crackers with a ripple of spiced cranberries. It was refreshing and vibrant, a perfect conclusion to a summer of transformation.

Since that memorable summer, icebox cakes have held a special place in my heart, reminding me of my P-Town summer family. We were young, carefree, and, above all, happy.

BUTTER PECAN ICEBOX CAKE

2 cups (240 g) pecans, chopped
¼ cup (56 g) salted butter
2 cups (480 g) heavy whipping cream
½ cup (56 g) powdered sugar
1 teaspoon vanilla extract
3 tablespoons real maple syrup
¼ teaspoon salt
1½ sleeves of Biscoff cookies (24 to 26 cookies)

1 Preheat your oven to 350°F. Line a sheet pan with parchment paper and spread the pecans evenly. Toast for 8 to 10 minutes, or until fragrant and lightly browned. Set aside to cool.

2 Once cooled, in a medium saucepan over medium heat melt the butter. Add the toasted pecans and cook, stirring frequently, for 3 to 4 minutes, or until the pecans are well coated and fragrant. Remove from the heat and let cool completely.

3 Meanwhile, in a large bowl with an electric hand mixer fitted with beater attachments, whip the heavy whipping cream, powdered sugar, vanilla, maple syrup, and salt until stiff peaks form. Fold half of the buttered pecans into the whipped cream.

4 Line a 9-by-5-inch loaf pan with plastic wrap, leaving an overhang on the sides.

5 Spread a thin layer of the maple whipped cream mixture on the bottom of the loaf pan.

6 Arrange a single layer of Biscoff cookies on top of the whipped cream, breaking them into pieces to fit if necessary.

7 Spread a layer of the maple whipped cream mixture over the cookies.

8 Continue layering cookies and whipped cream, ending with a layer of whipped cream on top. Sprinkle the remaining buttered pecans over the top.

9 Fold the overhanging plastic wrap over the top to cover completely. Refrigerate for at least 4 hours, or overnight, to allow it to set.

10 To serve, lift the icebox cake out of the pan using the plastic wrap overhang. Slice and enjoy!

ORANGE CREAMSICLE ICEBOX CAKE

½ cup (120 g) orange juice
¼ cup (60 g) orange zest
One 3.4-ounce package instant vanilla pudding mix
1½ cups (360 g) whole milk, cold
One 8-ounce package cream cheese, softened
½ cup (56 g) powdered sugar
1 teaspoon vanilla bean paste
1½ cups (360 g) heavy whipping cream
1 sleeve graham crackers (9 to 10 full cracker sheets)
Orange slices for garnish (optional)

1. Line a 9-by-5-inch loaf pan with plastic wrap, leaving an overhang on the sides.
2. In a medium bowl, whisk together the orange juice, zest, pudding mix, and cold milk until smooth. Chill in the refrigerator for 30 minutes.
3. Meanwhile, in a medium bowl with an electric hand mixer fitted with beater attachments, beat the cream cheese, powdered sugar, and vanilla together and mix until well combined.
4. In a separate medium bowl, whip the heavy cream until stiff peaks form. Fold the whipped cream into the cream cheese mixture.
5. To assemble the icebox cake, place a layer of graham crackers on the bottom of the prepared pan, breaking them to fit if necessary. Spread a layer of the cream cheese mixture over the graham crackers, followed by a layer of the orange pudding mixture. Repeat the layers, finishing with a layer of the cream cheese mixture on top.
6. Cover the loaf pan with plastic wrap and freeze for at least 4 hours, or overnight, to allow the cake to set.
7. To serve, remove the cake from the freezer and let set at room temperature for 30 minutes to thaw slightly. Then carefully remove the plastic wrap and invert the loaf pan onto a serving platter. Remove the pan and garnish the cake with the orange slices, if desired. Slice and serve cold.

COCONUT CREAM ICEBOX CAKE

One 3.4-ounce package instant white chocolate pudding mix

1½ cups (360 g) whole milk, cold

One 8-ounce package cream cheese, softened

½ cup (56 g) powdered sugar

1 teaspoon vanilla bean paste

1 teaspoon coconut extract

One 13½-ounce can coconut milk, chilled, thick cream part only

1½ (360 g) cups heavy whipping cream

1 sleeve graham crackers (9 to 10 full cracker sheets)

½ cup (40 g) sweetened shredded coconut

1 Line a 9-by-5-inch loaf pan with plastic wrap, leaving an overhang on the sides.

2 In a medium bowl, whisk together the pudding mix and cold milk until smooth. Chill in the refrigerator for 30 minutes.

3 Meanwhile, in a medium bowl with an electric hand mixer fitted with beater attachments, beat the cream cheese, powdered sugar, vanilla bean paste, coconut extract, and chilled coconut milk (only the thick cream part from the top of the can) until smooth and well combined.

4 In a separate medium bowl, using the electric hand mixer fitted with beater attachments, whip the heavy whipping cream until stiff peaks form. Fold into the cream cheese mixture.

5 To assemble the icebox cake, line the bottom of the prepared pan with a layer of graham crackers, breaking them to fit if necessary. Spread a layer of the cream cheese mixture over the graham crackers, followed by a pudding layer. Repeat the layers, finishing with a layer of the cream cheese mixture on top.

6 Cover the loaf pan with plastic wrap and refrigerate for at least 4 hours, or overnight, to allow the icebox cake to set.

7 To serve, carefully remove the plastic wrap and invert the loaf pan onto a serving platter. Remove the pan and top with toasted shredded coconut; slice and serve.

CHAPTER FOUR

CASSEROLE DISHES

While I cherish the recipes handed down to me by generations of blood family and chosen families, I also sincerely appreciate the concept of heirloom cookware. These are the cherished pieces collected over time by a succession of individuals, each one adding its perspective and memories long after the original owner is gone. Often, these relics are casserole dishes—Pyrex, thrift store finds, and oddly shaped vessels that bear the scars of wear and tear yet remain beautiful in their own right.

They come in various colors and patterns, serving as time capsules of the eras they were designed and made. When added to our home collections, they stand out and become the focal point of conversations, capturing the legacies of their previous owners.

More than just antiques, casserole dishes are versatile vessels. Their deep sides and generous capacity make them perfect for hosting some of the most decadent desserts. If the dish is glass, it can showcase the inner beauty of layered desserts like delights, puddings, and cobblers. Even a simple recipe using a few boxed ingredients can be elevated when served in an ornate dish. Casserole dish desserts are storytellers.

Growing up, I always felt drawn to these types of dishes. While they are typically associated with savory dishes, I saw their potential beyond the expected. In Long Beach, I witnessed their beauty in full spectrum, gathered on a table—each dish different yet collectively creating a beautiful scene, like a kaleidoscope of colors and the chapters of attendees' life stories. During a potluck, these desserts steal the show and hold the conversations.

When I think back to specific family recipes, I associate them with the dish they were served in. And though I have the recipes, unfortunately I don't have any of my family's treasured dishes. As a result, something is missing from the whole food-memory effect. Now, because I'm responsible for ensuring my son carries with him the recipes and food memories, I've started collecting these dishes to establish a home environment rooted in family values. I want to ensure that our stories, including those of our chosen family, are passed down to him and carried on for generations.

THE FOUR-LAYERED DESSERTS: DELIGHT, YUM-YUM, AND LUSH

I'VE HAD the chance to live in different parts of the country, from the West Coast to the East Coast, briefly in the Midwest, and now in the South. Each region has its own unique culture and culinary pride. One of the funniest debates I've come across is the friendly argument over the name of a certain layered pudding dessert. Depending on where you are, it might be called a delight, yum-yum, lush, or even dessert lasagna (which seems like a stretch to me).

Personally, I know these desserts as delights, so that's what I'll be calling them. But I respect the other names, and people's passion for their regional variations. A delight is a simple pleasure—a pudding dessert with layers of graham cracker crust, sweetened cream cheese, pudding, and whipped cream, topped with extra crumbs and fruit. It's sweet, unassuming, and perfect for warmer days and nights. But let me tell you, people can get surprisingly heated about them.

Before I started developing recipes professionally, I volunteered to help organize a community cookbook. (I do not recall the occasion, but I do remember that I just wanted to impress a friend whose mother was organizing the cookbook.) During the recipe selection process, I witnessed a woman throw a fit because a recipe was submitted for lemon lush, which she insisted should be called yum-yum. She argued that only recipes from longtime residents of her town should be included, and calling it anything else was disrespectful to the town's legacy.

It was a moment of realization for me. People can get so worked up over trivial things, but if we step back, we'll see that we have more in common than we think. The differences are often superficial, and there's more that unites us if we're willing to see it.

For the recipes in this book, I've included variations of these four-layered pudding desserts to suit everyone's taste. The Malt Chocolate Delight (page 171) takes some extra effort, as you need to infuse heavy cream with malt powder and chill it for at least 2 hours before whipping. I've also included a traditional Pistachio Delight (page 175) with mascarpone to balance the sweetness. My idea of a lush always involves crushed fruit or citrus, so I've added a Pineapple Coconut Lush (page 173). And for the yum-yum fans who swap pudding for pie filling, there's a blackberry version (page 178) reminiscent of the popular cherry yum-yum.

There's a dessert for everyone, but I encourage you to try them all and see that, despite the names and variations, they're all essentially the same—a delightful treat.

ENGLISH BREAKFAST TEA

MALT CHOCOLATE DELIGHT

FOR THE MALT WHIPPED CREAM LAYER

1⅓ cups (320 g) heavy whipping cream

¼ cup (40 g) malt powder

1 teaspoon vanilla bean paste

1 cup (113 g) powdered sugar

Dark or semi-sweet chocolate for garnish

FOR THE CHOCOLATE LAYER

Two 3.9-ounce packages instant chocolate pudding mix

4 cups (960 g) whole milk, cold

½ cup (75 g) malt powder

FOR THE CRUST

2 cups (240 g) graham cracker crumbs

½ teaspoon kosher salt

2 tablespoons granulated sugar

½ cup (113 g) unsalted butter, melted

FOR THE CREAM CHEESE LAYER

Two 8-ounce packages cream cheese, room temperature

1 cup (113 g) powdered sugar

2 tablespoons malt powder

8 ounces whipped topping

If you love malt chocolate candy, this dessert is perfect for you. The malt flavor shines in the malt whipped cream, and I also add malt to the chocolate pudding mix to ensure a harmonious blend between the layers. To make the malt whipped cream, it's crucial to chill the heavy whipping cream after infusing it with malt. Refrigerate it until completely cool, preferably overnight. This ensures the cream will whip to the desired stiffness. Chill the bowl in the freezer before whipping to further aid the process. The chocolate-malt flavors are bold yet balanced, and the salted buttery graham cracker crust provides a contrasting flavor and texture, making this delight irresistible.

1. Preheat the oven to 400°F and set aside a 9-by-13-inch casserole dish.

2. Make the whipped cream layer. In a small saucepan, whisk together vigorously the heavy cream and malt powder over medium-low heat until the malt is dissolved. Bring the mixture to a near boil; bubbles will form around the edges. Remove from the heat and pass the mixture through a fine mesh sieve into a sealable, heatproof container. Chill in the refrigerator for at least 2 hours.

3. Make the chocolate layer. In a medium bowl, whisk together the chocolate pudding, milk, and malt powder until evenly combined and the pudding and malt powder are dissolved. Cover with plastic wrap, placing the plastic wrap directly over the top of the pudding to prevent skin from forming. Chill in the refrigerator for at least 30 minutes to set.

4. Meanwhile, make the crust. In a separate medium bowl, whisk together the graham cracker crumbs, salt, and sugar. Add the butter and mix it with a fork until the mixture looks like wet beach sand, using the fork to break up any large clumps.
5. Pour the graham cracker mixture into the casserole dish and press it into an even layer on the bottom of the dish. Bake for 10 minutes; the crust will darken. Remove and cool completely on a wire rack. Don't touch the crust; it is delicate and will crack when still warm.
6. While the crust cools, make the cream cheese layer. In a medium bowl, using a hand mixer with beater attachments on medium-low speed, beat together the cream cheese, powdered sugar, and malt powder until combined and smooth. Add the whipped topping and continue beating until thoroughly combined.
7. To assemble, pour the cream cheese layer over the cooled crust and spread it into an even layer. Chill in the refrigerator for 30 minutes.
8. Remove the chocolate pudding from the refrigerator and stir it with a wooden spoon to loosen it. Pour the pudding over the cream cheese layer and spread it into an even layer. Return to the refrigerator and chill for another 30 minutes.
9. Remove the malt-infused heavy whipping cream from the refrigerator. Add the vanilla bean paste and powdered sugar. With an electric hand mixer, whip on medium-high speed until stiff peaks form, about 2 to 3 minutes.
10. Dollop the malt whipped cream over the pudding layer and spread it into an even layer. Using a fine grater, generously shave chocolate over the whipped cream. Serve cold immediately.

PINEAPPLE COCONUT LUSH

This lush is perfect for spring and even better for summer, bringing vacation vibes with its coconut-pineapple layers. Instead of vanilla pudding, I use white chocolate pudding mix, which adds a subtle rich and creamy flavor that complements the coconut and balances the acidity of the pineapple.

FOR THE WHITE CHOCOLATE PUDDING LAYER

Two 3.3-ounce packages instant white chocolate pudding mix

4 cups (960 g) whole milk, cold

One 20-ounce can crushed pineapple, drained

FOR THE CRUST

2 cups (240 g) graham cracker crumbs

½ teaspoon kosher salt

2 tablespoons granulated sugar

½ cup (113 g) unsalted butter, melted

FOR THE CREAM CHEESE LAYER

Two 8-ounce packages cream cheese, room temperature

1 cup (113 g) powdered sugar

1 teaspoon vanilla bean paste

One 8-ounce container whipped topping, thawed

FOR THE WHIPPED CREAM LAYER

2 cups (480 g) heavy whipping cream

½ cup (56 g) powdered sugar

2 teaspoons coconut extract

½ cup (40 g) sweetened shredded coconut, toasted, for garnish

1. Preheat your oven to 400°F and set aside a 9-by-13-inch casserole dish.

2. Make the chocolate pudding layer. In a medium bowl, whisk together the pudding mix and milk until evenly combined. Cover with plastic wrap, placing the plastic wrap directly over the top of the pudding to prevent skin from forming. Chill in the refrigerator to set.

3. Meanwhile, in a separate medium bowl, whisk together the graham cracker crumbs, salt, and sugar. Add the butter and mix it with a fork until the mixture looks like wet beach sand, using the fork to break up any large clumps.

4. Pour the graham cracker mixture into the casserole dish and press it into an even layer on the bottom of the dish. Bake for 10 minutes (the crust will darken). Remove and cool completely on a wire rack. Don't touch the crust; it is delicate and will crack when still warm.

5. While the crust cools, prepare the cream cheese layer. In a medium bowl, using an electric hand mixer on medium-low speed, beat together the cream cheese, powdered sugar, and vanilla bean paste until combined and smooth. Add the whipped topping and continue mixing until combined and smooth.

6. To assemble, pour the cream cheese layer over the cooled crust and spread it into an even layer. Chill in the refrigerator for 30 minutes.
7. Remove the white chocolate pudding from the refrigerator and stir it with a wooden spoon to loosen it. Fold in the pineapple. Pour over the cream cheese layer and spread it into an even layer. Return to the refrigerator and chill for another 30 minutes.
8. Meanwhile, prepare the whipped cream. In a medium bowl with an electric hand mixer, whip the heavy cream, powdered sugar, and coconut extract on medium-high speed until stiff peaks form, 2 to 3 minutes.
9. Dollop the whipped cream over the pudding layer and spread it into an even layer. Scatter toasted coconut evenly over the whipped cream layer. Place in the refrigerator until ready to serve.

PISTACHIO DELIGHT

FOR THE PUDDING LAYER

Two 3.4-ounce packages instant pistachio pudding mix

4 cups (960 g) whole milk

FOR THE CRUST

2 cups (240 g) graham cracker crumbs

½ teaspoon kosher salt

2 tablespoons granulated sugar

½ cup (113 g) unsalted butter, melted

FOR THE CREAM CHEESE LAYER

One 8-ounce package cream cheese

One 8-ounce package mascarpone

1 cup (113 g) powdered sugar

One 8-ounce container whipped topping, thawed

FOR THE WHIPPED CREAM LAYER

2 cups (480 g) heavy whipping cream

½ cup (56 g) powdered sugar

This dessert stays true to the original, with the simple addition of mascarpone to the cream cheese layer. The mascarpone adds a touch of tang and reduces the sweetness of the pistachio pudding. The cream cheese layer becomes slightly less sturdy with the mascarpone, so it may sink a bit when you spread the pistachio pudding on top. Just spread it slowly and evenly. The slight mixing of the two layers is intentional, so don't worry.

1. Preheat your oven to 400°F and set aside a 9-by-13-inch casserole dish.

2. Make the pudding. In a medium bowl, whisk together the pudding mix and milk until evenly combined. Cover with plastic wrap, placing the plastic wrap directly over the top of the pudding to prevent skin from forming. Chill in the refrigerator for at least 30 minutes to set.

3. Meanwhile, in a separate medium bowl, make the crust. Whisk together the graham cracker crumbs, salt, and sugar. Add the butter and mix it with a fork until the mixture looks like wet beach sand, using the fork to break up any large clumps.

4. Pour the graham cracker mixture into the casserole dish and press it into an even layer on the bottom of the dish. Bake for 10 minutes (the crust will darken). Remove and cool completely on a wire rack. Don't touch the crust; it is delicate and will crack when still warm.

5. While the crust cools, prepare the cream cheese layer. In a medium bowl, using an electric hand mixer on medium-low speed, beat together the cream cheese, mascarpone, and powdered sugar until combined and smooth. Add the whipped topping and continue mixing until combined and smooth.

6. To assemble, pour the cream cheese layer over the cooled crust and spread it into an even layer. Chill in the refrigerator for 30 minutes.

7. Remove the pistachio pudding from the refrigerator and stir it with a wooden spoon to loosen it. Pour over the cream cheese layer and spread it into an even layer. Return to the refrigerator and chill for another 30 minutes.

8. Meanwhile, prepare the whipped cream. In a medium bowl with an electric hand mixer, whip the heavy cream and powdered sugar on medium-high speed until stiff peaks form, 2 to 3 minutes.

9. Dollop the whipped cream over the pudding layer and spread it into an even layer. Place in the refrigerator until ready to serve.

BLACKBERRY YUM-YUM

FOR THE CRUST

2 cups (240 g) graham cracker crumbs

½ teaspoon kosher salt

3 tablespoons granulated sugar

½ cup (113 g) unsalted butter, melted

FOR THE CREAM CHEESE LAYER

One 8-ounce package cream cheese

1 cup (113 g) powdered sugar

½ teaspoon vanilla bean paste

1 cup (240 g) heavy whipping cream

Two 20-ounce cans blackberry pie filling, ¼ cup filling liquid reserved

FOR THE WHIPPED CREAM LAYER

2 cups (480 g) heavy whipping cream

1 cup (113 g) powdered sugar

¼ cup reserved blackberry filling liquid

The most common flavor for yum-yum is cherry, but you can use any pie-filling fruit. What you use depends on the season or your mood. I prefer blackberry because its bright flavor and bold purple hue contrast beautifully with the white cream cheese layer. Other flavors to consider are strawberry, apple, peach, and blueberry. No adjustments are needed—just swap out the blackberry for your chosen fruit.

1. Preheat your oven to 400°F and set aside a 9-by-13-inch casserole dish.
2. Make the crust. In a medium bowl, whisk together the graham cracker crumbs, salt, and sugar. Add the butter and mix it with a fork until the mixture looks like wet beach sand, using the fork to break up any large clumps.
3. Pour the graham cracker mixture into the casserole dish and press it into an even layer on the bottom of the dish. Bake for 10 minutes (the crust will darken). Remove and cool completely on a wire rack. Don't touch the crust; it is delicate and will crack when still warm.
4. While the crust cools, prepare the cream cheese layer. In a medium bowl, using an electric hand mixer on medium-low speed, beat together the cream cheese, powdered sugar, and vanilla bean paste until combined and smooth. Set aside.
5. In a separate medium bowl with an electric hand mixer on medium-high speed, whip the 1 cup heavy cream until stiff peaks form, 2 to 3 minutes. Fold the whipped cream into the cream cheese mixture until evenly combined.

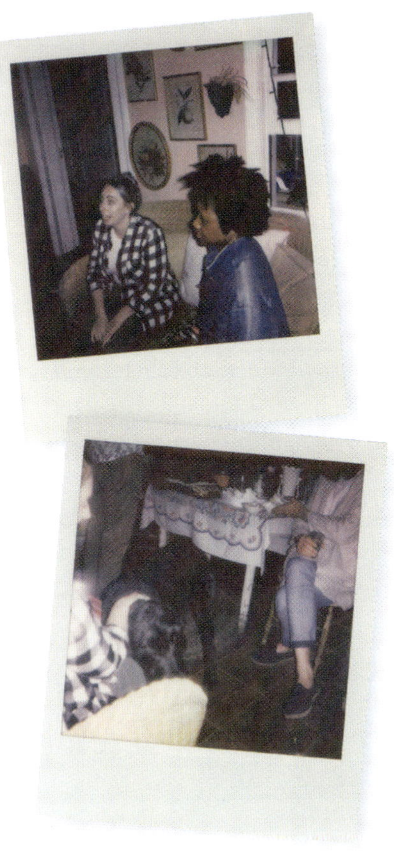

6 Pour the cream cheese layer over the cooled crust and spread it into an even layer. Chill in the refrigerator for 30 minutes.

7 Pour the pie filling over the cream cheese layer and spread evenly.

8 Prepare the whipped cream layer. In the same medium bowl used for the whipped cream previously, add the heavy whipping cream and powdered sugar. With an electric hand mixer on medium-high speed, whip until stiff peaks form. Dollop over the blackberry layer and spread into an even layer. Dollop the reserved blackberry filling randomly over the whipped cream. With the back of the spoon, swirl or swoosh filling into the whipped cream. Place in the refrigerator until ready to serve.

BROILED BANANA PUDDING

FOR THE PUDDING

6 egg yolks

⅓ cup (66 g) granulated sugar

3 tablespoons cornstarch

¼ teaspoon kosher salt

2 cups (280 g) whole milk

3 tablespoons unsalted butter, cold

1 teaspoon vanilla bean paste

FOR THE WHIPPED CREAM

1½ cups (360 g) heavy whipping cream

¼ cup (28 g) powdered sugar

Nilla Wafers, about 40 cookies

4 ripe bananas, peeled and sliced

FOR THE MERINGUE

6 egg whites

¼ teaspoon cream of tartar

¼ cup plus 1 tablespoon (67 g) granulated sugar

I've tried my fair share of banana puddings, but when I discovered broiled banana pudding, I was utterly hooked. The pudding itself is the same, but the charred, marshmallowy meringue topping takes it to another level. The charred topping adds a s'mores-like touch to the dessert, and the contrast of the cold pudding with the warm meringue is a delightful surprise with every bite.

Here's a tip: The pudding can be made ahead of time, but the meringue should be done just before serving to maintain its texture and torched appearance. Otherwise, you'll have a deflated meringue and a soft texture.

In my version, I use vanilla bean pudding (also known as pastry cream) folded into whipped cream for extra richness. However, if you prefer, you can use instant vanilla pudding—it's all delicious!

1. Prepare the pudding. In a medium bowl, whisk together the egg yolks, sugar, cornstarch, and salt until evenly combined, frothy, and pale yellow. Set aside.
2. In a medium saucepan over medium-low heat, add the milk and heat until just before boiling. Remove from the heat.
3. Carefully and slowly, pour the hot milk into the sugar-egg mixture, whisking continuously to temper the eggs. Once all the milk has been incorporated into the sugar-egg mixture, return the mixture to the saucepan. Over medium-low heat, stirring continuously with a wooden spoon to prevent the bottom from burning or the eggs cooking too fast, cook until the mixture thickens, 3 to 4 minutes. Don't bring to a boil. To test if it thickens enough, dip the spoon into the mixture and run your

finger down the back of the spoon and if the mixture doesn't run, the pudding is cooked. Remove from the heat and pour through a fine mesh sieve over a heat-proof bowl.

4 Stir in the butter and vanilla bean paste until melted and evenly combined. Cover with plastic wrap, placing it on top of the pudding to prevent a skin from forming; chill in the refrigerator for at least 1 hour or overnight.

5 Once the pudding is cooled, prepare the whipped cream. In a medium bowl with an electric hand mixer, whip the heavy cream and powdered sugar on medium-high speed until stiff peaks form. With a rubber spatula or wooden spoon, fold the whipped cream into the pudding until evenly combined. Set aside.

6 Assemble the banana pudding. In a 9-inch casserole dish, lay about 20 cookies in an even layer. Top the cookies with half of the banana slices. Pour half of the pudding over the bananas and evenly spread. Repeat the layers. Cover with plastic wrap and chill in the refrigerator for at least 1 hour or until ready to serve.

7 Prepare the meringue. In a medium bowl with an electric hand mixer on medium-high speed, whip together the egg whites and cream of tartar until soft peaks form, 1 to 2 minutes. Lower mixer to medium speed and slowly add the sugar, about 2 tablespoons at a time until fully incorporated; continue whipping until stiff peaks form and the mixture is glossy.

8 Dollop the meringue on the pudding and swoosh to make decorative peaks. Turn on the broiler in your oven and toast the meringue, rotating occasionally to toast evenly, until the meringue is set and toasted evenly. You can also use a kitchen torch if you have one. Carefully rotate periodically to ensure an even char.

9 Serve immediately.

Note: Keep the oven door slightly cracked open when broiling the meringue, watching carefully to make sure the meringue doesn't burn.

MIXED BERRY WHOLE WHEAT CRISP

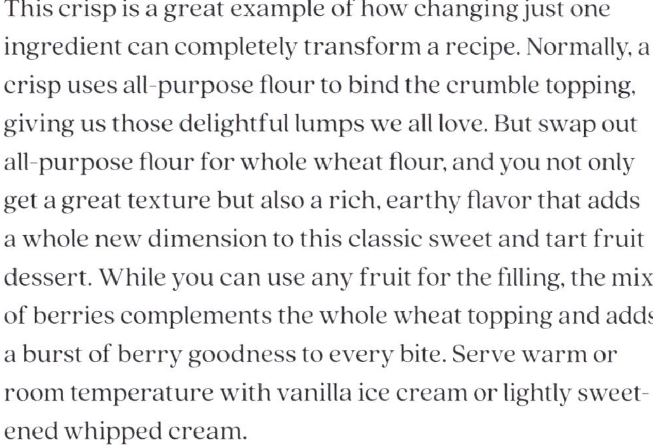

This crisp is a great example of how changing just one ingredient can completely transform a recipe. Normally, a crisp uses all-purpose flour to bind the crumble topping, giving us those delightful lumps we all love. But swap out all-purpose flour for whole wheat flour, and you not only get a great texture but also a rich, earthy flavor that adds a whole new dimension to this classic sweet and tart fruit dessert. While you can use any fruit for the filling, the mix of berries complements the whole wheat topping and adds a burst of berry goodness to every bite. Serve warm or room temperature with vanilla ice cream or lightly sweetened whipped cream.

FOR THE FRUIT FILLING

2 pounds frozen mixed berries, thawed and dried
½ cup (110 g) light brown sugar
2 tablespoons cornstarch
½ teaspoon ground cinnamon
¼ teaspoon ground cardamom
Juice of 1 lemon

FOR THE TOPPING

¾ cup (90 g) whole wheat flour
1 cup (90 g) old-fashioned oats
½ teaspoon kosher salt
1 teaspoon ground cinnamon
¼ cup (35 g) pecans, chopped
⅓ cup (73 g) light brown sugar
6 tablespoons unsalted butter, cold and cubed

1. Preheat your oven to 350°F and butter a 9-inch casserole dish. Set aside.
2. Make the fruit filling. In a medium bowl, add the mixed berries, brown sugar, cornstarch, cinnamon, cardamom, and lemon juice. Toss with your hands until evenly combined and the berries are coated. Pour into the prepared dish in an even layer. Set aside.
3. Prepare the topping. In a separate medium bowl, add the flour, oats, salt, cinnamon, pecans, and brown sugar. Whisk to combine evenly. Add the butter and with your hands, feather the butter into the dry ingredients until mixture looks shaggy.
4. Pour the topping over the berries and spread evenly; the topping should be a thick layer. Bake for 35 to 45 minutes, or until the berries are bubbling and the topping has darkened.

Note: To feather, squish the butter and dry ingredients between your fingers and slide fingers to combine the butter and dry ingredients together to resemble a feather.

FINDING YOURSELF IN

JASPER ARRIVED three weeks early, on a Wednesday evening, December 5, 2018, in Memphis, Tennessee. It was an emergency C-section, and since everything had been planned for every scenario with surrogacy, the decision between my ex-husband and me was made that I would go into the operating room if it came to that. I remember that night vividly. The operating room was painfully bright, and I felt disoriented. The medical team moved around with such precision that all I could focus on was the beeping of the machines. I was pacing, unsure of what to do, when I heard him cry. My immediate instinct was to reach for my baby. The nurse brought him over, weighed and measured him, wrapped him up, and handed him to me. I remember saying, "Oh, no!" and bursting into tears. In an instant, I went from thinking only of myself to thinking only of him. I became a parent in the blink of an eye.

I read that when your child is born, a chemical changes your hormones, rewires your brain, and triggers parental instincts. Whether it's scientifically proven or just a myth, I believe it. I can't explain how quickly my thoughts and actions changed. I was so focused on Jasper that I often needed to remember to care for myself. Parenthood, especially for first-timers, is challenging. I was navigating it based on instinct rather than reading "how to be a parent" books—I didn't have time for those. And there weren't many books for two dads expecting a baby.

Parenthood brought a whole new set of experiences. Time seemed to warp; we were living in newborn Jasper time. Simple tasks felt like rocket science; by day five, I had forgotten how to microwave bagel bites. I was constantly delirious, experiencing spontaneous emotions like crying or laughing at odd times. Most important, I was reliving infancy and childhood through Jasper's eyes. Everything that used to define me no longer mattered. Jasper was my priority then and now.

I embraced simplicity. Creating a warm, cozy home and building memories became my focus, replacing the controlled chaos and modern luxuries I once cherished. My main goal was to make a family.

But with new parenthood also came challenges. No matter the makeup of your family, parenthood is tough. Despite putting Jasper first and fostering a wholesome family environment and navigating a co-parent relationship, I needed more support than I realized. Parenthood introduced me to a

PARENTHOOD

new kind of chosen family—not a group of like-minded people collectively caring for each other, but individuals who stepped in when I needed help the most.

Neighbors I had barely met left gifts for Jasper and food for me when they heard we had just welcomed our son home. They offered childcare when I had appointments or needed a break. They became a sounding board for my parenting worries and stories of exhaustion, reassuring me that I was doing well.

Even strangers, like my realtors at the time, took the time to understand my struggles and offered support. Social media friends became a source of comfort, allowing me to share my thoughts without the pressure of being physically present due to childcare limitations.

This period in my life, though brief, felt like a lifetime. I was stripped to the core, exposed for not knowing what I was doing or who I was. I felt alone, and yet strangers showed up, not my closest friends, family, or established network. It was people I had never met or people I only knew on a surface level.

This experience shifted my perspective on life, I now focused on Jasper as my top priority, and it also changed how I viewed my career. I love baking, but I needed to catch up on where it all began: in my home, for the people I love. I had let social expectations influence my approach to baking, using ingredients and techniques that didn't align with why I chose baking as a career. During this transition time, I went back to basics. With little income, minimal free time, and a burning desire to bake for my new family, I rediscovered myself.

RASPBERRY BUCKLE

12 ounces raspberries
1¼ cups (265 g) plus 1 tablespoon granulated sugar
1¼ cups (156 g) all-purpose flour
½ teaspoon baking powder
½ teaspoon baking soda
1 teaspoon kosher salt
2 eggs
1 teaspoon vanilla paste
Zest of 1 lemon
2 tablespoons buttermilk
½ cup (113 g) unsalted butter, melted
Powdered sugar, garnish

Picture a buckle as the coffee cake's playful cousin in the world of cobblers. It's a charming mound of fruit folded into a cake-like batter or generously sprinkled on top, leading to the batter "buckling" around it as it bakes. While you can use any fruit you fancy, raspberries are a prime choice thanks to their size—which allows for maximum buckle—and their vibrant, refreshing burst of flavor. Serve with lightly sweetened whipped cream or vanilla ice cream.

1. Preheat the oven to 325°F and butter a 9-inch casserole dish. Set aside.
2. In a small bowl, toss the raspberries with 1 tablespoon of the sugar until evenly coated. Set aside.
3. In a separate small bowl, whisk together the flour, baking powder, baking soda, and salt until evenly combined.
4. In a medium bowl, whisk together the eggs, 1¼ cups sugar, vanilla paste, zest, buttermilk, and butter until evenly combined. Fold in the dry ingredients with a wooden spoon or rubber spatula until just combined with a few visible flour streaks.
5. Pour the batter into the prepared dish and smooth it into an even layer. Evenly scatter the raspberries and their juices over the batter. Bake for 45 to 50 minutes, or until golden brown and a toothpick or cake tester inserted in the middle comes out clean. Remove and set on a wire rack; let cool for 5 to 10 minutes.
6. With a fine mesh sieve, dust the buckle with powdered sugar; serve warm.

CHOCOLATE STRAWBERRY COBBLER

FOR THE STRAWBERRIES

- 1½ pounds strawberries (about 4 cups), hulled and sliced
- ½ cup (100 g) granulated sugar
- 3 tablespoons cornstarch
- ½ teaspoon vanilla extract

FOR THE TOPPING

- 1 cup (125 g) all-purpose flour
- ½ cup (100 g) granulated sugar
- ¼ cup (21 g) unsweetened cocoa powder
- 2 teaspoons baking powder
- ½ teaspoon kosher salt
- ½ cup (120 g) whole milk
- 6 tablespoons unsalted butter, melted
- 1 teaspoon vanilla extract
- ½ cup (87 g) dark chocolate chips

I used to think of cobbler as a straightforward vanilla buttery batter affair, but that all changed when a friend brought his chocolate strawberry cobbler to a party. His version was like a molten lava cake with syrupy strawberries instead of oozing hot fudge in the center. The chocolate was dark, not overly sweet, and incredibly rich. The fresh strawberries added a bright contrast, balancing out the richness perfectly. It was my first real lesson in how balance can elevate a dessert. This recipe aims for the same balance—decadent dark chocolate topping paired with a bright, slightly sweet strawberry center, creating a sensation reminiscent of indulging in a chocolate-covered strawberry. Serve with vanilla ice cream or lightly sweetened whipped cream.

1. Preheat your oven to 350°F and butter a 9-inch casserole dish. Set aside.
2. In a medium bowl, add the strawberries, sugar, cornstarch, and vanilla. Toss with your hands until evenly combined and the strawberries are coated. Pour into the prepared dish and spread into an even layer.
3. Prepare the topping. In a separate medium bowl, whisk together the flour, sugar, cocoa powder, baking powder, and salt until evenly combined. Make a well in the center of the dry ingredients. Add the milk, butter, and vanilla to the center of the well and whisk until evenly combined. Fold in the chocolate chips.
4. Pour the topping over the strawberries and spread slightly in an even layer. Bake for 20 to 30 minutes, or until the strawberries are bubbling and the topping looks dry. Serve warm or room temperature.

SNICKERDOODLE PEACH COBBLER

FOR THE PEACHES

2 pounds frozen peaches, thawed and towel-dried
½ cup (100 g) granulated sugar
2 tablespoons cornstarch
1 teaspoon ground cinnamon
¼ teaspoon ground nutmeg
¼ teaspoon ground cardamom
¼ teaspoon kosher salt
Juice of ½ lemon

FOR THE SNICKERDOODLE TOPPING

1½ cups (187 g) all-purpose flour
½ teaspoon cream of tartar
½ teaspoon baking soda
¼ teaspoon salt
½ cup (113 g) unsalted butter, softened
½ cup (120 g) granulated sugar, plus 3 tablespoons for coating
¼ cup (55 g) light brown sugar
1 egg
1 teaspoon vanilla extract
1 teaspoon ground cinnamon for coating

They say the name "cobbler" comes from the cobbled look of dropped dough, resembling stone pathways. Whether that's true or not, it's a fitting image. You can re-create this effect by placing cookie dough over the fruit before baking.

For this cobblestone effect, you'll need a cookie dough that spreads while baking and complements the fruit's flavors. Snickerdoodles work wonders for stone fruit or apple cobblers, and my personal favorite is peach.

In this cobbler, a thick peach syrup bubbles up around the snickerdoodles' crispy edges. As you dig in, you'll hear that satisfying crack as the spoon meets the cookie. The combination of sweet, juicy peaches and the cinnamon-sugar goodness of snickerdoodles is simply irresistible. Serve with vanilla ice cream or lightly sweetened whipped cream.

1 Preheat your oven to 375°F and butter a 9-by-13-inch casserole dish. Set aside.

2 Prepare the peaches. In a medium bowl, add the peaches, sugar, cornstarch, cinnamon, nutmeg, cardamom, salt, and lemon juice. Toss with your hands until evenly combined and the peaches are coated. Pour into the prepared dish and spread into an even layer.

3 Prepare the snickerdoodle topping. In a medium bowl, whisk together the flour, cream of tartar, baking soda, and salt until evenly combined. Set aside.

4 In a separate medium bowl with an electric hand mixer, cream the butter, ½ cup of the sugar, and brown sugar until light and fluffy, 2 to 3 minutes. Add the egg and vanilla and beat until evenly combined. Add the dry ingredients to butter-sugar mixture and mix until just combined, with a few flour streaks visible.

5 In a small bowl, whisk together the remaining 3 tablespoons sugar and 1 teaspoon cinnamon until evenly combined. With an ice cream scoop, scoop the dough and roll into a ball. Coat the dough in the cinnamon-sugar mix and place over the peaches randomly. Repeat until all the dough is used.

6 Bake for 15 minutes. Remove from the oven and with the bottom of a 1-cup measuring cup, slightly flatten the partially baked dough. Return to the oven and continue baking for 15 to 20 minutes, or until the peaches are bubbling and the cookies have flattened and crackled. Serve warm or room temperature.

PLUM SLUMP

FOR THE PLUMS

10 to 12 large plums, pitted and sliced
½ cup (100 g) granulated sugar
1 tablespoon lemon juice
½ teaspoon ground cinnamon
¼ teaspoon ground nutmeg
¼ teaspoon salt
1 cup (240 g) water

FOR THE TOPPING

2 cups (250 g) all-purpose flour
½ cup (100 g) granulated sugar
1 tablespoon baking powder
½ teaspoon salt
½ cup (113 g) cold unsalted butter, cut into small pieces
1 cup (240 g) buttermilk

The cobbler family is vast, with many variations of this humble dessert. One of its lesser-known members is the slump. It's a charming dish where the fruit is cooked slightly on the stovetop before being topped with a biscuit-like dough. The whole thing is then cooked on the stovetop or in the oven. The fruit bubbles up as it cooks, and the biscuits rise, absorbing the warm fruit and "slumping" into the sauce. It's like the chicken and dumplings of the dessert world!

I particularly enjoy slumps because the fruit tends to become a little jammy rather than saucy, and the topping is more delicate and fluffier than that of their sturdier, cakey cobbler cousins. Serve topped with vanilla ice cream.

1 Preheat your oven to 375°F and butter a 9-inch casserole dish. Set aside.

2 Prepare the plums. In a large heavy-bottom pan, combine the plums, sugar, lemon juice, cinnamon, nutmeg, salt, and water. Bring to a simmer over medium heat, stirring occasionally. Simmer for 5 to 7 minutes, or until the plums are slightly softened and the sugar has dissolved. Remove from the heat.

3 Make the topping. In a large bowl, whisk together the flour, sugar, baking powder, and salt until combined. Add the butter, using your fingers to work the butter into the dry ingredients until the mixture resembles coarse crumbs. Make a well in the center and add the buttermilk. Slowly mix together with your hands; the mixture will be thick and sticky.

4 Pour the plum mixture into the prepared pan. Drop spoonfuls of the batter over the plums, covering as much of the surface as possible.

5 Bake for 35 to 40 minutes, or until the topping is golden brown and the plum mixture is bubbling.

6 Remove from the oven and let it cool for a few minutes before serving. Serve warm.

APPLE SONKER WITH "MILK DIP"

FOR THE APPLES

2 pounds apples, about 8 cups
½ cup (100 g) granulated sugar
½ cup (110 g) light brown sugar
1 tablespoon ground cinnamon
¼ teaspoon ground ginger
¼ teaspoon ground clove
¼ teaspoon ground nutmeg
½ teaspoon kosher salt
2 tablespoons cornstarch
Juice of 1 lemon

FOR THE BATTER

2 cups (250 g) all-purpose flour
¼ cup (50 g) granulated sugar
2 teaspoons baking powder
½ teaspoon kosher salt
1¾ cups (420 g) buttermilk
1 egg
1 teaspoon vanilla bean paste
¼ cup (57 g) unsalted butter, melted

FOR THE "MILK DIP"

4 egg yolks
½ cup (100 g) granulated sugar
1½ teaspoons vanilla bean paste
1 cup (240 g) heavy whipping cream

My mother hails from North Carolina, where cobbler goes by a different name—sonker. Originating in Surry County, North Carolina, the sonker has many variations, depending on the family. Some pour a batter into a dish and add fruit on top, like an inverted pie, while others lay pie-like dough over the fruit. My favorite version involves baking fruit in a dish until it cooks down and thickens, then pouring a pancake-like batter over the hot fruit and baking until golden brown.

What sets a sonker apart is its milk dip—a sweetened milk sauce poured over the dessert, bringing all the flavors together. In my version, inspired by my time in North Carolina, I stick to the pancake-like batter for the topping. To balance the flavors, I break down the sonker into three components: fruit for acid and spice; batter for buttery notes; and a "milk dip" for sweetness.

The milk dip is essentially an Americanized version of French crème anglaise, so I opted to make an anglaise; hence, "milk dip" in quotation marks. Making this "milk dip" is simple, and it completes the sonker with a sweet vanilla payoff.

1 Preheat your oven to 350°F. Spray a 9-inch casserole dish with baking spray. Set aside.

2 Prepare the apples. Peel the apples and slice into ¼-inch pieces. Place in a medium bowl and add the sugars, cinnamon, ginger, clove, nutmeg, salt, and cornstarch. Using your hands, toss the apples and evenly coat them with sugar, spices, and cornstarch. Add the lemon juice and toss.

3 Pour the apples into the prepared dish and spread evenly. Apples will heap over the dish, which is okay as

they will cook down. Bake for 40 minutes, or until the sauce thickens and bubbles, checking occasionally and stirring with a wooden spoon, scraping the bottom.

4 Make the batter. Meanwhile, add the flour, sugar, baking powder, and salt to a separate medium bowl and whisk together to combine thoroughly.

5 Make a well in the center of the flour mixture and add the buttermilk, egg, vanilla paste, and melted butter. Fold the dry ingredients into the wet ingredients using a rubber spatula until combined. A few lumps will be present, and that's okay.

6 Once the apples are cooked down and the sauce is bubbling, remove the dish from the oven and carefully pour the batter over the apples, spreading evenly with a rubber spatula.

7 Return to the oven and bake for another 20 minutes, or until golden brown and a toothpick or cake tester inserted in the middle comes out clean. Remove from oven and cool.

8 As the sonker cools, make the "milk dip." In a small bowl, whisk together the egg yolks, sugar, and vanilla paste until combined and have a paste consistency.

9 Add the heavy cream to a medium saucepan and bring to a simmer over medium-low heat; don't bring to a boil.

Note: The heavy cream should be warm enough for bubbles to form around the edges. But watch that it doesn't boil!

10 Immediately remove the pan from the heat and carefully and slowly pour half the heavy cream into the sugar-yolk mixture while whisking continuously. Whisk vigorously until combined. Continue adding the remaining heavy cream and whisking until combined.

11 Return the mixture to the saucepan and cook it over low heat, stirring continuously with a wooden spoon and scraping the bottom of the pan. Avoid bringing to a boil. "Milk dip" is cooked when the mixture coats the back of the spoon. To test, dip the spoon in the mixture, turn the back of the spoon toward you, and run your finger lengthwise. The mixture should be firm enough not to run.

12 To serve, spoon the sonker into a bowl and pour "milk dip" over the sonker.

MELT-IN-YOUR-MOUTH CASHEW FUDGE

FOR THE FUDGE

- ½ cup (62 g) cashew halves, lightly salted
- ½ cup (113 g) unsalted butter
- One 7-ounce jar marshmallow creme
- 1 cup (250 g) creamy cashew butter
- 1 teaspoon vanilla extract
- 2 cups (225 g) powdered sugar, sifted

FOR THE GANACHE

- ¼ cup (60 g) heavy whipping cream
- 1 tablespoon unsalted butter
- ½ cup (87 g) dark chocolate chips
- ⅓ cup (45 g) cashew halves, lightly salted

This recipe is a nod to my family's love for peanut butter fudge, which was always around but devoured at record speed. However, I could only handle a piece or two before the rich, thick confection became too much. Not being the biggest fan of peanut butter but a fan of fudge, here I've opted for my favorite type of nut and a softer nut butter—cashew.

This fudge is less dense than peanut butter fudge, offering a delicate, melt-in-your-mouth texture. The saltiness of the cashews perfectly balances the sweetness of the marshmallow creme and chocolate coating. The fudge is very soft, and folding in cashew halves adds just enough texture to each bite and helps hold the fudge together. You can cut it into squares or rectangular bars, or you can wrap it in parchment paper for a grab-and-go treat.

1. Prepare the fudge. Spray an 8-by-8-inch casserole dish with baking spray and line with parchment paper. Set aside. Roughly chop the cashews and set aside.
2. In a small saucepan over medium-low heat, melt the butter and marshmallow creme until combined, stirring constantly. Once combined, turn off the heat, but leave the saucepan on the stovetop. Stir in the cashew butter and vanilla until evenly combined.
3. Once the cashew butter is combined, slowly add the powdered sugar, stirring vigorously until smooth and combined. The mixture will be lumpy, but continue stirring; it will smooth out. Fold in the cashews.

4 Pour into the prepared pan and spread into an even layer. Cover lightly with plastic wrap and chill in the refrigerator until set, about 30 minutes.

5 Once the fudge is set, make the chocolate ganache. In a small saucepan over medium-low heat, bring the heavy whipping cream to a simmer; do not boil it.

6 Remove from the heat and whisk in the butter and chocolate until they are melted and evenly combined. Fold in the cashews.

7 Pour the ganache over the chilled fudge and spread it evenly. Return the fudge to the refrigerator and chill for 1 hour. Portion the fudge; serve on a platter or store it in an airtight container.

From top: Bumpy Road Cereal Bars (page 75), Melt-In-Your-Mouth Cashew Fudge (page 199), and Ambrosia Salad (page 247)

"DUMP" CAKES

In my teens and early 20s, I practically lived on dump cakes—those one-stop-shop desserts where you just mix a boxed cake mix with fruit and butter, dump it all in a pan, and bake without any fuss. I knew I had to include a version of these cakes in my cookbook, but replicating that exact approach proved to be a challenge.

Instead, I decided to put a twist on two of my favorite cakes: pineapple upside-down cake and German chocolate cake. I created versions where the traditional techniques, for example, the layering of pineapple in the pineapple upside-down cake or the intricate frosting of the German chocolate cake, are set aside. Instead, everything is simply "dumped" into the pan and baked, resulting in delicious cakes that are easy to make and even easier to enjoy.

GERMAN CHOCOLATE "DUMP" CAKE

FOR THE CAKE

2 cups (250 g) all-purpose flour
2 cups (400 g) granulated sugar
¾ cup (63 g) unsweetened cocoa powder
2 teaspoons baking powder
1½ teaspoons baking soda
1 teaspoon kosher salt
1 cup (240 g) buttermilk
½ cup (100 g) vegetable oil
2 large eggs
2 teaspoons vanilla extract
½ cup (120 g) hot brewed coffee

FOR THE COCONUT TOPPING

1 cup (240 g) evaporated milk
1 cup (200 g) granulated sugar
½ cup (113 g) unsalted butter
3 egg yolks
1 teaspoon vanilla extract
1 cup (115 g) pecans, chopped
1⅓ cups (115 g) sweetened shredded coconut

1 Preheat your oven to 350°F. Spray a 9-by-13-inch casserole dish with baking spray. Set aside.

2 Prepare the cake. In a medium bowl, whisk together the flour, sugar, cocoa powder, baking powder, baking soda, and salt. Make a well in the center.

3 Add the buttermilk, vegetable oil, eggs, and vanilla to the center of the dry ingredients and whisk together until evenly combined. Carefully stir in the hot coffee until the batter is smooth.

4 Pour the batter into the prepared pan. Set aside.

5 Prepare the coconut topping. In a medium saucepan over medium-low heat, add the evaporated milk, sugar, butter, egg yolks, and vanilla, whisking continuously until the mixture starts to thicken, about 10 minutes. Remove from the heat and fold in the pecans and coconut.

6 Pour the topping over the batter and bake for 30 to 40 minutes, or until a toothpick or cake tester inserted in the middle comes out clean with a few crumbs. Remove from the oven and cool on a wire rack. Serve warm or room temperature.

PINEAPPLE UPSIDE-DOWN "DUMP" CAKE

FOR THE CAKE

1½ cups (187 g) all-purpose flour, sifted
1 cup (200 g) granulated sugar
2 teaspoons baking powder
½ teaspoon kosher salt
½ cup (120 g) pineapple juice
½ cup (120 g) whole milk
6 tablespoons unsalted butter, melted
1 egg
1 teaspoon vanilla bean paste

FOR THE SAUCE

½ cup (113 g) unsalted butter
1 tablespoon pineapple juice
¾ cup (165 g) dark brown sugar
One 20-ounce can pineapple tidbits
One 10-ounce jar sliced maraschino cherries, drained

1. Preheat your oven to 350°F. Spray a 9-by-13-inch casserole dish with baking spray. Set aside.
2. Prepare the cake. In a medium bowl, whisk together the sifted flour, sugar, baking powder, and salt until evenly combined. Make a well in the center of the dry ingredients.
3. Add the pineapple juice, milk, butter, egg, and vanilla bean paste to the center of the well and whisk until evenly combined. Pour the batter into the prepared dish.
4. Prepare the sauce. In a medium saucepan over medium-low heat, add the butter, pineapple juice, and brown sugar. Whisk continuously until the butter melts and the sugar dissolves. Add the pineapple tidbits and cherries and stir to combine.
5. Pour the sauce over the batter and bake for 35 to 45 minutes, or until a toothpick or cake tester inserted in the middle comes out clean with a few crumbs. Remove from the oven and cool on a wire rack. Serve warm or room temperature.

COCONUT-LIME SELF-SAUCING PUDDING

FOR THE PUDDING

1 cup (125 g) all-purpose flour

½ cup (40 g) unsweetened shredded coconut

½ cup (100 g) granulated sugar

2 teaspoons baking powder

¼ teaspoon kosher salt

½ cup (112 g) canned coconut milk

½ cup (120 g) heavy whipping cream

Juice and zest of 2 limes

¼ cup (56 g) unsalted butter, melted

1 teaspoon vanilla bean paste

¼ teaspoon coconut extract

FOR THE SAUCE

½ cup (100 g) granulated sugar

½ cup (120 g) boiling water

½ cup (112 g) canned coconut milk

Juice and zest of 1 lime

¼ teaspoon coconut extract

When I got married for the first time, the wedding was an absolute blast. About 100 of our closest friends were there, making it a proper celebration with our chosen families. Our Boston crew made up the biggest group. Even though the marriage didn't last, I still fondly recall that day. It was all about the sheer joy and happiness of being together, just celebrating each other. Those are the memories I've chosen to hold on to!

One of the highlights of the wedding was the milk and cookie bar, and my favorite treat was a coconut-lime shortbread. I loved those flavors so much that I used them to create this self-saucing pudding. As it bakes, the sauce transforms into a texture similar to curd. The dessert is vibrant and zesty, hitting all the right notes for a summer gathering. It's my way of honoring that magical night and the bond we all shared. It also serves as a reminder that relationships evolve naturally; it's how we adapt to those changes that matter most.

1 Preheat your oven to 350°F and butter a 9-inch casserole dish. Set aside.

2 Prepare the pudding. In a medium bowl, whisk together the flour, coconut, sugar, baking powder, and salt. Make a well in the center of the dry ingredients. Add the coconut milk, heavy cream, lime juice, lime zest, melted butter, vanilla bean paste, and coconut extract to the center of the well. Whisk together until evenly combined. Pour the mixture into the prepared dish and spread evenly.

continues

3 Prepare the sauce. In a small bowl, whisk together the sugar, boiling water, coconut milk, lime zest, lime juice, and coconut extract until evenly combined. Pour the sauce over the pudding mixture. Do not stir.

4 Bake for 25 to 30 minutes, or until the top of the pudding is lightly golden brown and the sauce is bubbling up around the edges.

5 Remove from the oven and let it cool for a few minutes before serving.

ORANGE-TOFFEE SELF-SAUCING PUDDING

FOR THE PUDDING

1 cup (125 g) all-purpose flour
½ cup (100 g) granulated sugar
1 teaspoon baking powder
½ teaspoon kosher salt
½ teaspoon ground cinnamon
¼ teaspoon ground nutmeg
2 tablespoons unsalted butter, melted
½ cup (120 g) whole milk
Zest of 1 orange
1 teaspoon vanilla extract

FOR THE SAUCE

1 cup (220 g) light brown sugar
1 cup (240 g) boiling water
2 tablespoons unsalted butter
1 teaspoon vanilla extract

This recipe is my only call-out to the holiday season in this book. I've always loved that time of year, but it took me a while to feel truly comfortable with the holidays, especially since I wasn't spending them with my blood family. For many in the LGBTQIA+ community, the holidays can be tough because they have so much emphasis on family. It's a constant reminder for those of us who can't be with our families despite wanting to be there so badly.

I've had several holidays where I had no plans, and the generosity and care of friends who invited me to their homes truly saved me during some of my saddest, most lonely times. Their kindness was a beacon of light during a season of perpetual hope.

This recipe is a nod to toffee self-saucing pudding but with a twist of warm holiday flavors like orange. A tradition I grew up with was making orange pomanders (oranges studded with cloves) and bringing a little bit of my childhood home to my new home results in a fragrant, rich, and delicious dessert that pairs perfectly with vanilla ice cream, which adds a creamy texture to the pudding.

1 Preheat your oven to 350°F and butter a 9-inch casserole dish. Set aside.

2 Prepare the pudding. In a medium bowl, whisk together the flour, sugar, baking powder, salt, cinnamon, and nutmeg. Make a well in the center of the dry ingredients. Add the butter, milk, orange zest, and vanilla to the center of the well. Whisk together until evenly combined. Pour the mixture into the prepared dish and spread evenly.

continues →

3. Prepare the sauce. In a medium bowl, whisk together the brown sugar, boiling water, butter, and vanilla extract until the sugar is dissolved and the mixture is smooth. Set aside. Pour the sauce over the pudding mixture. Do not stir.
4. Bake for 25 to 30 minutes, or until the top of the pudding is golden brown and the sauce is bubbling up around the edges.
5. Remove from the oven and let it cool for a few minutes before serving.

BRÛLÉED BREAD PUDDING WITH BUTTERSCOTCH SAUCE

FOR THE BREAD PUDDING

16 cups (about 2 loaves) stale bread (such as brioche, challah, or pullman), cubed about 1 inch

4 cups (960 g) whole milk

⅔ cup (132 g) granulated sugar

1 tablespoon ground cinnamon

2 teaspoons ground cardamom

½ teaspoon kosher salt

5 eggs

2 teaspoons vanilla bean paste

FOR THE BRÛLÉE TOPPING

¼ cup (57 g) unsalted butter, room temperature

¼ cup (50 g) granulated sugar

FOR THE BUTTERSCOTCH SAUCE

1 cup (220 g) light brown sugar

½ cup (165 g) light corn syrup

3 tablespoons unsalted butter

1½ teaspoons kosher salt

½ cup (120 g) heavy whipping cream

1 tablespoon plus 1 teaspoon brandy (optional)

I used to work at a restaurant where we always had extra bread at the end of the night. It felt like such a waste, especially since there was a limit of how many bread crumbs we could make out of it. So I decided to take a chance and make bread pudding, but not just any bread pudding—a small batch, off-menu version that depended on the amount of leftover bread from the night before.

And if I was going to make bread pudding, I would do it my way. I didn't want the typical mushy, overly soaked bread pudding. Instead, I aimed for something with texture, something inspired by Thanksgiving stuffing but with a sweet twist. I created a custard, infused with cinnamon and cardamom, that was just right for soaking the bread and binding it together but that left the top to crisp up beautifully. Then, I brûléed it with a generous amount of sugar, creating a sweet, caramelized crust.

This bread pudding is a flavor explosion, served warm and topped with a light but bold butterscotch sauce. And if you can, serve it with a scoop of buttermilk or sweet cream ice cream (page 156) for the perfect finishing touch.

1 Butter a 15-inch casserole dish and add the bread to the dish (bread will be heaping over the dish).

2 In a medium bowl, whisk together the milk, sugar, cinnamon, cardamom, salt, eggs, and vanilla bean paste until evenly combined. Pour the custard over the bread, then firmly press down on the bread to absorb the custard and compress the bread into an even layer. All the bread

should be pressed down far enough to absorb the custard. Cover with foil and chill in the refrigerator for at least 30 minutes, best overnight.

3 Preheat your oven to 350°F. Leave the bread pudding covered with the foil and bake for 35 to 40 minutes, or until the bread pudding puffs up and when pressed down no custard rises from the center or around the edges.

4 Remove from the oven and discard the foil. Make the brûlée topping. With an offset spatula or rubber spatula, carefully spread the butter over the top of the bread, then sprinkle with sugar. Raise the oven rack two notches down from the top of the oven and set your oven to broil. Place the bread pudding back in the oven and broil until the sugar is caramelized with a deep amber color, rotating the dish a few times for an even caramelization, 2 to 3 minutes. You can also use a kitchen torch if you have one. Remove the bread pudding and cool on a wire rack.

5 Meanwhile, prepare the butterscotch sauce. In a medium saucepan over medium-low heat, whisk together the brown sugar, corn syrup, butter, and salt. Bring the mixture to a boil, lower the heat, and continue boiling for 3 minutes, continuing to whisk to prevent scorching on the bottom. Whisk in the heavy cream and continue cooking for 1 minute. Remove from the heat and pour through a fine mesh sieve over a heatproof bowl to collect any burnt pieces. Whisk in the brandy, if using.

Note: Butterscotch can be made 3 days ahead and stored in an airtight container in the refrigerator. Reheat in a saucepan over low heat and bring back to just a boil.

6 Serve the bread pudding warm. Scoop a serving into a bowl and pour a generous helping of butterscotch over the top.

CHAPTER FIVE

BOWLS, BUNDTS, AND OTHER ROUND THINGS

Round bakeware offers a departure from the structured nature of rectangular pans or sheet pans, inviting a different kind of creativity. These curved vessels encourage us to break free from the constraints of straight edges and right angles, and to embrace the natural flow of curves and circles. In round bakeware, we discover the freedom to layer flavors and textures in ways that surprise and delight.

Circular dishes are fluid, free forms that transcend rigid lines. They allow us to experiment with traditional forms, reinventing them into something new and introducing fresh perspectives. These vessels often contain some of the most intriguing desserts at potlucks, such as dessert salads like ambrosia and fluff salad. These colorful creations blur the lines between dessert and side dish, existing in their own category and defying traditional categorization.

Circular bakes possess a certain unruliness; without the confines of strict edges, they bake as they please, adding an element of unpredictability to the baking process. No matter how we try to contain them, they seem to have a mind of their own.

L. W.'S SWEET TEA POUND CAKE

FOR THE TEA CREAM

1 cup (240 g) heavy whipping cream
2 large black tea bags

FOR THE POUND CAKE

3 cups (375 g) all-purpose flour
¼ teaspoon baking soda
2 cups (454 g) unsalted butter, softened
2 cups (400 g) granulated sugar
8 eggs
1 teaspoon vanilla extract
2 teaspoons lemon zest

FOR THE SIMPLE SYRUP

1 cup (240 g) water
1 cup (200 g) granulated sugar
5 large black tea bags

FOR THE GLAZE

1⅓ cups (153 g) powdered sugar
2 tablespoons lemon juice
1 teaspoon lemon zest

My husband, Louis, is a true Southern gentleman in my eyes. He's got a charming accent, a knack for storytelling, a love for family time, and a talent for creating lasting memories. When I asked him what recipe he'd like to see in this cookbook, he suggested a sweet tea pound cake. It wasn't a childhood favorite or a cherished family recipe; he simply thought it sounded delicious. But it was a fantastic idea, so we worked on it together, and it made its way into the book. It may not have a long history, but it's special to us because it's the first recipe we collaborated on. To infuse the cake with black tea flavor, we steep tea bags in heavy whipping cream. The infused cream is then added to the batter. For an extra tea kick, we make tea simple syrup to brush over the warm cake after baking. And to top it off and enhance that sweet tea flavor, the pound cake is finished with a lemon glaze.

1. Preheat your oven to 350°F and set aside a 10-cup bundt pan.
2. Prepare the tea cream. In a medium saucepan over medium-low heat, add the heavy cream and bring to just before boiling. Little bubbles will form around the edges when it is hot but not boiling. Turn off the heat and add the tea bags. Cover and let steep for 15 minutes. Discard the tea bags and set the cream aside.
3. Prepare the cake. In a medium bowl, sift together the flour and baking soda. Set aside.

continues

4. In a medium bowl with an electric hand mixer, cream the butter and sugar together until light and fluffy, 5 to 7 minutes. With the mixer on low speed, add the eggs one at a time and mix well before adding the next egg.
5. Stop the mixer and add the tea cream, vanilla, and zest. Mix together until smooth and evenly combined.
6. Stop the mixer and add the flour mixture in two additions, sifting for a second time into the wet ingredients. Mix on low speed until just combined. Finish mixing by hand with a rubber spatula or wooden spoon.
7. Generously spray the bundt pan with baking spray and pour the batter into the pan. Tap the pan a few times on the counter to release any air bubbles. Bake for 60 to 70 minutes, or until golden brown and a toothpick or cake tester inserted in the middle comes out clean. Cool on a wire rack for 30 minutes.
8. Meanwhile, make the simple syrup. In a small saucepan over medium heat, add the water and sugar. Stir and bring to boil until the sugar is dissolved. Turn off the heat and add the tea bags. Steep for 5 minutes. Discard the tea bags. Set aside the simple syrup.
9. Place a plate or platter upside down over a slightly cooled pound cake. Carefully invert and remove the pan. With a pastry brush, generously brush the simple syrup over the entire cake. Repeat the step every 5 minutes until the simple syrup is gone.
10. Prepare the glaze. In a small bowl, whisk together the powdered sugar, lemon juice, and lemon zest until evenly combined.
11. Once the cake is cool to the touch, pour the glaze over the pound cake. Let set before serving.

ACTUAL COFFEE, COFFEE CAKE

FOR THE COFFEE STREUSEL

¼ cup (50 g) unsalted butter
1 tablespoon instant coffee powder
¾ cup (165 g) light brown sugar
2 teaspoons ground cinnamon
3 tablespoons all-purpose flour
1 cup (100 g) pecans, chopped
¼ teaspoon kosher salt

FOR THE CAKE

2 cups (240 g) cake flour
2 cups (250 g) all-purpose flour
1 teaspoon kosher salt
4 teaspoons baking powder
2 teaspoons baking soda
½ cup (100 g) vegetable oil
½ cup (113 g) unsalted butter
1½ cups (300 g) granulated sugar
2 eggs
1 tablespoon vanilla extract
2 cups (480 g) buttermilk
Powdered sugar for garnish

One of Del Martin and Phyllis Lyon's early events, Gab 'n' Java, was a gathering where women came together over coffee and cake. To honor their legacy and the spirit of communal gathering, I created a coffee cake with actual coffee in it. It's also a tribute to those early Gab 'n' Javas in 1950s San Francisco. Unlike traditional coffee cakes with a streusel topping, this one only has a cinnamon-sugar ribbon marbled throughout its interior. By infusing melted butter with instant coffee powder, the ribbon becomes a burst of coffee flavor. During baking, it slowly sinks from the top to the center, creating a sticky, gooey texture and a super moist crumb with a robust coffee flavor. Enjoy this cake for an extra jolt in the morning or when guests come over. You never know what one gathering among a chosen family can lead to—it might just change the world.

1 Preheat your oven to 350°F. Set aside a 10-cup bundt pan (do not grease the pan until ready to add the batter).

2 Prepare the coffee streusel. In a small bowl, whisk together the melted butter and instant coffee until dissolved and evenly combined.

3 In a medium bowl, add the brown sugar, cinnamon, flour, pecans, and salt and stir together to evenly combine. Add the coffee-butter mixture and with a fork, mix together to evenly combine and form crumbles. Set aside.

4 Prepare the cake. In a separate medium bowl, whisk together the flours, salt, baking powder, and baking soda until evenly combined. Set aside.

continues →

5 In a separate medium bowl with an electronic hand mixer, cream the oil, butter, and sugar together until evenly combined and smooth, 1 to 2 minutes. Add the eggs and vanilla and mix until evenly combined.

6 Gradually add the dry ingredients to the wet ingredients, alternating with the buttermilk until smooth and well combined.

7 Generously spray the bundt pan with baking spray and pour the batter into the pan. Carefully tap the pan to make sure all the batter is in the crevices of the bundt pan and no air bubbles are present. Top with the streusel, scattering evenly over the top.

8 Bake for 40 to 50 minutes, or until a toothpick or cake tester inserted in the middle comes out clean. Cool on a wire rack for 20 minutes in the pan. Place a plate or platter upside down over the bundt and carefully invert the cake. Remove the pan and let the cake continue to cool completely. Dust with powdered sugar and serve.

Note: The streusel will sink into the middle of the cake when it bakes; don't be discouraged if the top of the cake looks cracked—remember, it's actually the bottom once it's inverted.

BOOZY COCONUT RUM BUNDT CAKE (BOOM! CAKE)

FOR THE CAKE

2 cups (250 g) all-purpose flour
1 teaspoon baking powder
½ teaspoon baking soda
½ teaspoon kosher salt
½ cup (120 g) sour cream
½ cup (120 g) whole milk
½ cup (120 g) coconut rum
1 cup (227 g) unsalted butter, softened
1½ cups (335 g) granulated sugar
4 eggs
1 teaspoon vanilla bean paste

FOR THE GLAZE

½ cup (113 g) unsalted butter
¼ cup (60 g) water
1 cup (200 g) granulated sugar
½ cup (120 g) coconut rum

This rum cake is a legend in my Boston family, affectionately known as boom! cake. The name comes from a hilarious mishap involving our friend Will, who was making a big batch of his family's rum cake recipe for a party. Will accidentally multiplied the recipe quantities in an Excel spreadsheet, resulting in a cake that was insanely boozy.

When we arrived at the party, Will was still glazing the cake with its sweet rum mixture. The glazing process can take a while even with the correct quantities, because the layers need to slowly soak into the cake. But with the miscalculated recipe, it took hours. We watched as Will set and reset a timer to douse the cake, unaware of the impending alcohol onslaught.

Once the cake was finally ready, we all took a bite before Will did—and were nearly knocked off our feet by the intense boozy flavor. But instead of letting on, we kept it to ourselves. When Will finally tried a bite, he realized his mistake, and the boom! cake was born.

Despite its explosive beginnings, this cake is now a beloved treat. It's still boozy, but it has just the right amount to give you a pleasant buzz rather than knock you out. Serve plain or with lightly sweetened whipped cream.

1. Preheat your oven to 350°F. Set aside a 10-cup bundt pan.
2. Prepare the cake. In a medium bowl, whisk together the flour, baking powder, baking soda, and salt. Set aside.
3. In a small bowl, whisk together the sour cream, milk, and rum until evenly combined. Set aside.

continues

The longer Boom! Cake sets, the more the rum glaze soaks in, enhancing its rich, boozy flavor.

4 In a separate medium bowl with an electric hand mixer, cream the butter and sugar together until light and fluffy, 2 to 3 minutes. Add the eggs and vanilla bean paste and mix until evenly combined, 1 minute.

5 Gradually add the dry ingredients to the butter-sugar ingredients, alternating with the milk-rum until smooth and well combined.

6 Generously spray the bundt pan with baking spray and pour the batter into the pan. Carefully tap the pan to make sure all the batter is in the crevices of the bundt pan and no air bubbles are present.

7 Bake for 35 to 45 minutes, or until a toothpick or cake tester inserted in the middle comes out clean. Cool on a wire rack for 10 minutes in the pan. Place a plate or platter upside down over the bundt and carefully invert the cake. Remove the pan and let the cake continue to cool.

8 Meanwhile, prepare the glaze. In a small saucepan over medium heat, stir together the butter, water, and sugar until the butter is melted. Bring to a boil, reduce the heat to low, and simmer for 5 minutes. Remove from the heat and whisk in the rum.

9 With a pastry brush, generously brush the glaze over the entire cake. Let rest for 10 minutes and repeat until all the glaze has been used.

BLUEBERRY-LIME BUNDT CAKE

FOR THE BLUEBERRY RIBBON

1 pint fresh blueberries
2 tablespoons granulated sugar
1 tablespoon water
1 tablespoon cornstarch

FOR THE CAKE

2 cups (250 g) all-purpose flour
1 teaspoon baking powder
½ teaspoon baking soda
½ teaspoon kosher salt
½ cup (120 g) sour cream
½ cup (120 g) whole milk
1 cup (200 g) granulated sugar
Zest of 2 limes
½ cup (113 g) unsalted butter, room temperature
2 eggs
1 teaspoon vanilla bean paste

FOR THE GLAZE

1⅓ cups (153 g) powdered sugar
2 tablespoons lime juice
1 teaspoon lime zest
1 tablespoon plus 1 teaspoon whole milk

The first thing I ever baked was a batch of blueberry muffins. I must have been around eight, with the kitchen all to myself and just a hint of adult supervision. Despite turning the batter a vivid shade of purple from too many frozen blueberries, the muffins were delicious! Blueberry muffins became my signature bake, a tradition I carried on until I moved away. These days, I prefer my blueberries in cake form, especially for brunch. This Bundt cake celebrates my love for abundance and is loaded with a thick blueberry ribbon that runs through the middle. To add a zesty kick, I mix lime zest into the batter and then finish the cake with lime icing once it's completely cooled.

1. Preheat your oven to 350°F. Set aside a 10-cup Bundt pan.
2. Prepare the blueberry ribbon. In a medium saucepan over medium-low heat, add the blueberries, sugar, water, and cornstarch. Stir occasionally to prevent scorching and bring to just a boil. Mixture is done when the blueberries burst and the sauce thickens. Set aside.
3. Prepare the cake. In a medium bowl, whisk together the flour, baking powder, baking soda, and salt. Set aside.
4. In a small bowl, whisk together the sour cream and milk until evenly combined. Set aside.
5. In a separate medium bowl, add the sugar and lime zest and rub together with your fingers until evenly combined. With an electric hand mixer, cream the butter

continues

and lime-sugar together until light and fluffy, 2 to 3 minutes. Add the eggs and vanilla and mix until evenly combined, about 1 minute.

6 Gradually add the dry ingredients to the butter-egg ingredients, alternating with the sour cream-milk mixture until smooth and well combined.

7 Generously spray the Bundt pan with baking spray and pour half the batter into the pan. Carefully tap the pan to make sure the batter is in the crevices of the Bundt pan and no air bubbles are present. Pour the blueberry ribbon evenly over the batter. Pour the remaining batter over the blueberry ribbon and evenly smooth.

8 Bake for 35 to 45 minutes, or until a toothpick or cake tester inserted in the middle comes out clean. Cool on a wire rack for 20 minutes in the pan. Place a plate or platter upside down over the Bundt and carefully invert the cake. Remove the pan and let the cake continue to cool.

9 Meanwhile, prepare the glaze. In a small bowl, whisk together the powdered sugar, lime juice and zest, and milk until evenly combined. Once the cake is completely cooled, pour the glaze over the Bundt and let set before serving.

HOT MILK CAKE WITH CHOCOLATE GANACHE

FOR THE CAKE

2 cups (250 g) all-purpose flour
2½ teaspoons baking soda
1¼ teaspoons kosher salt
4 eggs
2 teaspoons vanilla extract
2 cups (400 g) granulated sugar
1 cup (240 g) whole milk
¾ cup (170 g) unsalted butter

FOR THE GANACHE

1 cup (175 g) semi-sweet chocolate chips
¾ cup (180 g) heavy cream

When I think about home baking, hot milk cake comes to mind. It's a classic recipe in which hot milk and butter are added to the batter, resulting in a cake rich in buttery, vanilla, and slightly caramel flavors with a dense yet tender crumb.

This recipe dates back to the 19th century, and the focus is more on technique than fancy ingredients or elaborate presentation. The method used in this cake is a trick I use in other cake recipes, and it's a tried-and-true method that always works.

Hot milk cake has no signature topping; some prefer it plain, while others like to dust it with powdered sugar or serve it with fruit compote. I love to top it with a thick chocolate ganache. The ganache drips down the sides, creating a stunning contrast with the blonde cake shaped by the Bundt pan. It's a simple cake with looks that steal the show.

1 Preheat the oven to 350°F.

2 Make the cake. In a medium bowl, whisk together the flour, baking soda, and salt until well combined. Set aside.

3 In another medium bowl, whisk the eggs and vanilla until the eggs are fully broken. Continue whisking and gradually add the sugar, vigorously whisking in some to combine before adding more sugar. Continue until all the sugar is added and the mixture doubles, almost triples, in size. Set aside.

continues

4 In a small saucepan over medium heat, combine the milk and butter. Heat the milk and melt the butter, swirling the pan a few times to prevent the milk from scalding on the bottom. Remove from the heat when the butter is completely melted and the milk is warm but not boiling.

Note: When tiny bubbles start forming around the pan's edges, the milk is warm.

5 Alternating between the flour mixture and the milk-butter mixture, add in thirds to the sugar-egg mixture. Fold the mixture gently with a wooden spoon or rubber spatula, being careful not to deflate the air whisked into the eggs.

6 Grease a 10-cup Bundt pan with baking spray, making sure to coat the crevices of the pan. Pour the batter into the pan and bake for 30 to 35 minutes, or until golden brown and a cake tester or toothpick inserted in the middle comes out clean.

7 Immediately and carefully, invert the cake onto a wire rack lined with parchment paper (this prevents the warm cake from sticking to the wire rack) and remove the pan. Let the cake cool completely before frosting.

8 When the cake is completely cool, make the ganache. Place the chocolate in a small bowl. Heat the heavy cream in a medium saucepan over medium heat until just before boiling. Look for small bubbles around the edge of the pan. Immediately pour the hot cream over the chocolate and whisk until the chocolate is completely melted, smooth, and shiny.

9 Transfer the ganache to a small heatproof measuring glass and let it sit for another 10 minutes to cool and thicken slightly.

10 Once thickened, pour the ganache over the cake, ensuring that the top of the cake is covered and allowing the ganache to drip down the sides. Let the chocolate firm up for at least 1 hour before serving.

CONFETTI ANGEL FOOD CAKE

- 1 cup (120 g) cake flour
- 1½ cups (300 g) granulated sugar
- 12 large egg whites, room temperature
- 1 teaspoon cream of tartar
- ¼ teaspoon kosher salt
- 1 teaspoon vanilla bean paste
- ½ cup (80 g) rainbow sprinkles

We've got a treasure trove of kitchen tools from Louis's grandmother, including her trusty tube pan. I adore the little dings and the slight color changes that tell stories of its years spent in her kitchen. Louis often shares warm memories of his grandmother, which revolve around cooking or baking. It's heartwarming to see how he cherishes those memories, much like I do with my chosen family tales. This angel food cake is a celebration, a way to honor Louis's grandmother's legacy, and a chance to add a modern touch to a classic so that Jasper can continue to tell the story of this pan. Serve confetti angel food cake with slightly sweetened whipped cream and extra sprinkles!

1. Preheat your oven to 350°F and have an ungreased 10-inch tube pan ready.
2. In a medium bowl, sift together the cake flour and ¾ cup (150 g) of the sugar. Set aside.
3. In a large bowl with an electric hand mixer with the beater attachments attached, beat the egg whites on medium speed until foamy. Add the cream of tartar and salt and continue beating until soft peaks form, 2 to 3 minutes.
4. With the mixer on, gradually add the remaining ¾ cup (150 g) of sugar, about 2 tablespoons at a time, beating on high speed until stiff peaks form.

Note: Not all rainbow sprinkles are the same, so when you fold them in some of the color could bleed, creating streaks in the batter or changing the batter a light purple hue.

5 Gently fold in the vanilla bean paste and rainbow sprinkles until just combined. Sprinkle the flour mixture over the egg white mixture, about ¼ cup at a time, folding in gently after each addition.

6 Spoon the batter into the ungreased tube pan and smooth the top with a spatula. Bake for 40 to 45 minutes, or until the top is golden brown and the cake springs back when lightly touched.

7 Remove the cake from the oven and invert the pan onto a cooling rack. Let the cake cool completely in the pan, then remove it from the pan.

BLUEBERRY UPSIDE-DOWN CORN CAKE

FOR THE CAKE

1¼ cups (156 g) all-purpose flour
¼ cup plus 1 tablespoon (50 g) cornmeal
2 teaspoons baking powder
¼ teaspoon kosher salt
¼ teaspoon cream of tartar
1 cup (200 g) granulated sugar
3 eggs
1 teaspoon vanilla bean paste
½ cup (133 g) sour cream
½ cup (100 g) vegetable oil

FOR THE BLUEBERRIES

¼ cup (56 g) unsalted butter
¼ cup (55 g) dark brown sugar
1 pint blueberries
2 teaspoons lemon zest

This cake is my go-to when I have new friends over who have yet to taste my baking. It's a great way to showcase my style in the kitchen—introducing new flavor combinations to classic recipes while keeping the sweetness in check and letting other flavors shine. This cake is a winner every time, and it's inspired by my love for pineapple upside-down cake.

I first made this cake for a potluck event years ago, where the theme was for chefs to bring dishes that represented their cooking style. It was an actual potluck experience, leading me to some of my closest friends to this day. Instead of a traditional yellow cake base, I use a corn cake base. The blueberries are caramelized on the stovetop before being poured into the pan, ensuring that all the sugar is dissolved and every blueberry is coated in caramel. When selecting blueberries, the smaller the berries, the better, as the smaller size ensures no bare cake is showing. I recommend serving this cake warm, preferably with a generous scoop of No-Churn Buttermilk Ice Cream (page 155) or No-Churn Sweet Cream Ice Cream (page 156), or slightly sweetened whipped cream.

1 Preheat your oven to 350°F. Line the bottom of a 10-inch springform pan with parchment paper, then press the ring down and latch to secure. Set aside.

2 Prepare the cake. In a medium bowl, whisk together the flour, cornmeal, baking powder, salt, cream of tartar, and sugar. Make a well in the center of the dry ingredients.

continues

3 Add the eggs, vanilla bean paste, sour cream, and oil to the center of the well and whisk together until evenly combined. Set aside.

4 Prepare the blueberries. In a medium saucepan over medium heat, stir together the butter and brown sugar until the butter is melted and the sugar is dissolved. Add the blueberries and lemon zest and continue cooking until the blueberries soften, stirring to coat the blueberries, 4 to 6 minutes. Pour the mixture into the prepared springform pan.

5 Pour the batter over the blueberries and spread evenly. Bake for 30 to 40 minutes, or until golden brown and a toothpick or cake tester inserted in the middle comes out clean. Cool on a wire rack for 10 minutes. Carefully unlatch the ring and remove. Place a plate or platter upside down over the cake and carefully invert. Remove the pan and parchment and let the cake continue to cool. Serve warm or room temperature.

GENEVA'S TRIFLE RULEBOOK

Geneva's presence was like a ray of sunshine. No matter how bad your day was, the moment she walked in, the room would light up and you'd forget all your troubles. She had this incredible perspective in which everything was just wonderful, and her radical optimism was contagious. I found myself wanting to embody that same energy.

She always seemed to have trifles ready, as if she knew guests would show up unexpectedly. They were either already waiting or she'd disappear into the kitchen and come out moments later with a tray of cocktails and a trifle dish in hand.

I finally asked her about the trifles, and with a smirk, she admitted that she never had them prepared in advance. She would simply throw together whatever she had on hand—leftover desserts or pantry staples—and create something new, "reincarnating ingredients," as she put it. I couldn't believe I hadn't thought of that party trick myself. From then on, whenever I'm in a pinch in the kitchen, I ask myself, "What would Geneva make?"

These trifles are inspired by Geneva's approach, using pantry staples and recipes from this cookbook to create something new. Think of these three trifles as guides or inspiration and then get creative with your own versions. Just remember Geneva's trifle rulebook: Include something with crumbs, whip up some heavy cream in seconds, add some fruit for a healthy touch, give it a crunch, and if it's after 10 AM, feel free to add some booze. Everything else is up to you!

BANANA SPLIT TRIFLE

1 Banana Fudge Snacking Cake recipe (page 79), minus the fudge frosting
2 cups (480 g) heavy whipping cream
½ cup (56 g) powdered sugar
1 teaspoon vanilla bean paste
3 to 4 ripe bananas, sliced
One 20-ounce can crushed pineapple, drained
1 cup (150 g) strawberries, hulled and chopped
½ cup (160 g) strawberry preserves
1 cup (240 g) chocolate sauce or hot fudge sauce
Maraschino cherries for garnish
Chopped nuts for garnish (optional)

1 Prepare the banana cake. Once baked and cooled, cut into 1- to 2-inch cubes.

2 In a large bowl with an electric hand mixer with beater attachments attached, whip the heavy whipping cream, powdered sugar, and vanilla bean paste together until stiff peaks form.

3 In a trifle dish or large glass bowl, layer half of the cake cubes on the bottom.

4 Top the cake layer with half of the sliced bananas, half of the crushed pineapple, and half of the chopped strawberries.

5 Spoon half of the strawberry preserves over the fruit layer. Spread half of the whipped cream over the strawberry layer. Drizzle half of the chocolate sauce over the whipped cream. Repeat the layers, reserving leftover whipped cream and chocolate sauce for garnishing.

6 Cover and refrigerate the trifle for at least 2 hours or until ready to serve.

7 Right before serving, top the trifle with the remaining whipped cream and chocolate sauce. Garnish with maraschino cherries and chopped nuts, if desired.

BUTTERSCOTCH TRIFLE

- 1 Butterscotch Sauce recipe from Brûléed Bread Pudding (page 211)
- Two 3½-ounce packages cook and serve butterscotch pudding mix
- 4 cups (960 g) whole milk
- ½ cup (110 g) light brown sugar
- ¼ cup (56 g) unsalted butter
- 1¼ cups (300 g) heavy whipping cream
- ½ teaspoon kosher salt
- ¼ cup (28 g) powdered sugar
- 1 teaspoon vanilla extract
- 2 pounds pound cake, cut into 1- to 2-inch cubes
- Butterscotch chips for garnish (optional)

1. Prepare the butterscotch sauce. Once made, let it cool until ready to use.
2. In a medium saucepan over medium heat, stir together the butterscotch pudding mix and milk, stirring constantly, and bring to a boil. Transfer to a heatproof bowl, cover the top of the pudding with plastic wrap to prevent skin from forming, and chill for at least an hour.
3. Meanwhile, in a medium saucepan over medium heat, combine the brown sugar, butter, ¼ cup (60 g) of the heavy whipping cream, and salt. Stir constantly until the mixture comes to a boil. Boil for 1 minute, then remove from the heat and let cool slightly.
4. In a medium bowl with an electric hand mixer with the beater attachments attached, whip the remaining 1 cup (240 g) heavy whipping cream, powdered sugar, and vanilla together until stiff peaks form.
5. In a trifle dish or large glass bowl, layer half of the cake cubes on the bottom. Pour a third of the butterscotch sauce over the cake. Then a layer of pudding, then a layer of whipped cream. Repeat layers.
6. Cover and refrigerate the trifle for at least 2 hours or until ready to serve.
7. Before serving, top the trifle with the remaining butterscotch sauce and sprinkle with butterscotch chips, if using.

BLACK FOREST TRIFLE

- Chocolate Cherry Soda Cake (page 145), doubled, without frosting
- One 21-ounce can cherry pie filling
- ¼ cup (60 g) cherry brandy (optional)
- 2 cups (480 g) heavy whipping cream
- ½ cup (56 g) powdered sugar
- 1 teaspoon vanilla extract
- ½ cup (42 g) unsweetened cocoa powder
- 1 cup (175 g) dark chocolate chips, chopped
- Dark chocolate bar for garnish

1. Prepare the chocolate cherry soda cake, doubling the recipe and baking in a 9-by-13-inch pan for 30 to 35 minutes, or until a toothpick inserted in the middle comes out clean. Once baked and cooled, cut into 1- to 2-inch cubes.
2. In a small bowl, stir together the cherry pie filling with the cherry brandy, if using.
3. In a large bowl using an electric hand mixer with the beater attachments attached, whip the heavy whipping cream, powdered sugar, vanilla, and cocoa powder until stiff peaks form.
4. To assemble the trifle, layer half of the chocolate cake cubes in the bottom of a trifle dish or large glass bowl.
5. Spoon half the cherry mixture over the cake, then spread half the chocolate whipped cream over the cherries. Sprinkle half of the chopped chocolate chips over the whipped cream. Repeat the layers.
6. Cover and refrigerate the trifle for at least 2 hours to allow the flavors to meld.
7. Right before serving, garnish with dark chocolate shavings.

MANDARIN ORANGE CHEESE PIE

FOR THE CRUST

2 cups (240 g) graham cracker crumbs

¼ cup (50 g) granulated sugar

¼ teaspoon kosher salt

½ cup (113 g) unsalted butter, melted

FOR THE FILLING

Two 8-ounce packages cream cheese

¼ cup (28 g) powdered sugar

One 14-ounce can sweetened condensed milk

1 teaspoon vanilla bean paste

Pinch of kosher salt

One 15-ounce can mandarin oranges, drained

FOR THE TOPPING

½ cup (120 g) heavy whipping cream

1 orange, zest only

I have a soft spot for no-bake desserts, but sometimes they can be misleading. Many recipes call for a premade cookie crust, which is delicious, but let's be real—it was baked at some point to set that crust. So when a recipe requires you to make the crust from scratch and then chill it in the fridge, you miss out on that toasty, baked flavor a crust gets after a few minutes in the oven.

So, is this truly a no-bake recipe? Well, kind of. You do need to turn the oven on for 10 minutes to bake the crust. But everything else is made without any heat. The pie is a twist on cheesecake, but it's much smoother and less dense, with a milder tang. The mandarin oranges add a burst of freshness, but be gentle when folding them in—they're delicate and can break down quickly if you're too rough.

If you can bear to have your oven on for just 10 minutes, I recommend making this pie. The moments of heat are totally worth it for the delicious result!

1. Preheat your oven to 400°F and set aside a 10-inch springform pan.
2. Prepare the crust. In a medium bowl, whisk together the graham cracker crumbs, sugar, and salt until evenly combined. Add the butter and with a fork, mix together until evenly combined and the mixture looks like wet beach sand.
3. Using the bottom of a 1-cup measuring cup, press the mixture into the bottom of the springform pan. Bake for 10 minutes. Place on a wire rack and cool completely.

Dogs are always welcome at a potluck!

4 Meanwhile, prepare the filling. In a medium bowl with an electric hand mixer, cream together the cream cheese and powdered sugar until light and fluffy, 2 to 3 minutes. Add the condensed milk, vanilla bean paste, and salt and mix until evenly combined and mixture is smooth and creamy, 1 to 2 minutes. Gently fold in the mandarin oranges, being careful not to break them down, until evenly distributed.

5 Pour the filling over the cooled crust and spread evenly. Loosely cover with plastic wrap and chill in the refrigerator for at least 4 hours, best overnight.

6 Before serving, in a medium bowl with an electric hand mixer on medium-high speed, whip the heavy cream until stiff peaks form, 2 to 3 minutes. Spread over the center of the pie, making sure not to cover the crust's edges. With a fine grater, zest the orange over the whipped cream. Serve chilled.

Broiled Banana Pudding
(page 181)

Peanut Butter and Roasted Red Grape Cheesecake Squares (page 67)

From left: Pistachio Fluff Salad (page 248), Confetti Angel Food Cake (page 229), and Whole Wheat Chocolate Chip Cookie Bars with Salted Vanilla Frosting (page 88)

AMBROSIA SALAD

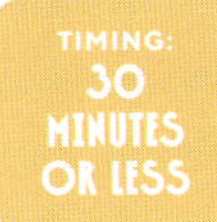

Potlucks just wouldn't be the same without ambrosia, the iconic "salad" that's a staple among church ladies. It's a classic, no doubt about it. I don't know who first came up with it, but I'd hug them if I could. However, in true queer fashion, even ambrosia deserves a little glow-up. The changes here are simple. Instead of using whipped topping, I whip up a mixture of cream cheese, vanilla bean paste, and heavy whipping cream for a thicker, creamier base. I also toast the coconut and walnuts for an extra depth of flavor, and I rinse the maraschino cherries to keep the white base from turning pink. These minor adjustments dial down the sweetness and elevate ambrosia to a new level.

- One 8-ounce package cream cheese
- ½ cup (28 g) powdered sugar
- 1 teaspoon vanilla bean paste
- 1½ cups (360 g) heavy whipping cream
- Two 8-ounce cans pineapple tidbits, drained
- ½ cup (40 g) shredded sweetened coconut, toasted
- 1 cup (50 g) mini marshmallows
- ½ cup (60 g) walnuts, toasted and chopped
- One 15-ounce can mandarin oranges, drained
- One 10-ounce jar sliced maraschino cherries, drained and rinsed

1. In a medium bowl with an electric hand mixer, cream together the cream cheese, powdered sugar, and vanilla bean paste until light and fluffy, 2 to 3 minutes.
2. In a separate medium bowl with an electric hand mixer, whip the heavy cream until stiff peaks form, 1 to 2 minutes. With a rubber spatula, fold the whipped cream into the cream cheese mixture until evenly combined.
3. Fold in the pineapple until evenly combined. Repeat the step for the remaining ingredients in the following order: coconut, marshmallows, walnuts, mandarin oranges, and finishing with the maraschino cherries.
4. Transfer the ambrosia to a serving bowl, wrap with plastic wrap, and chill in the refrigerator until ready to serve.

Note: The flavors will continue to develop the longer it chills; the best is overnight.

PISTACHIO FLUFF SALAD

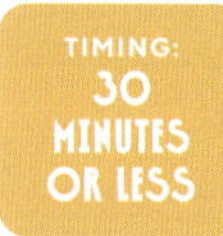

Two 3.4-ounce packages instant pistachio pudding

Two 8-ounce cans crushed pineapple

One 7-ounce jar marshmallow creme

¾ cup (180 g) sour cream

1½ cups (360 g) heavy whipping cream

2 cups (200 g) mini marshmallows

Don't let the seafoam green color fool you; give this fluff salad a chance. Known as pistachio fluff salad or Watergate salad, it has a bit of an urban legend surrounding its origins. Some claim it was created as a political protest or satire. However, it was actually born in 1975, the same year instant pistachio pudding hit the market.

The classic version includes instant pudding, pineapple, whipped topping, marshmallows, and nuts. My take keeps the instant pistachio pudding but swaps whipped topping for marshmallow creme, adds unsweetened heavy whipping cream and sour cream to balance the sweetness, uses crushed pineapple for a colorful pop, and foregoes the nuts. Trust me, it's worth a try!

1. In a medium bowl with a rubber spatula, stir together the pudding mix and pineapple until evenly combined and the pudding mix is dissolved. The mixture will be very thick. Fold in the marshmallow creme and sour cream until evenly combined. Set aside.
2. In a separate medium bowl with an electric hand mixer, whip together the heavy cream until stiff peaks form, 1 to 2 minutes. Fold the whipped cream into the pudding-pineapple mixture until evenly combined. Fold in the mini marshmallows.
3. Transfer the pistachio fluff to a serving bowl, wrap with plastic wrap, and chill in the refrigerator until ready to serve.

Note: The flavors will continue to develop the longer it chills; the best is overnight.

CRANBERRY-ORANGE FLUFF SALAD

Not all fluff salads are alike. While some tend to be super sweet, this cranberry-orange variation offers a more subdued, mellow flavor profile. It's bright and acidic, almost serving as a palate cleanser, which is a nice change of pace. It works as a dessert, but I love serving it as a side dish for a meal, making it a great alternative to traditional cranberry relish.

- One 8-ounce package cream cheese
- ¾ cup (85 g) powdered sugar
- One 14-ounce can whole cranberry sauce
- 1½ cups (360 g) heavy whipping cream
- ⅔ cup (80 g) pecans, toasted and chopped
- 2 cups (200 g) mini marshmallows
- One 15-ounce can mandarin oranges, drained

1. In a medium bowl with an electric hand mixer, cream together the cream cheese and powdered sugar until light and fluffy, 2 to 3 minutes. Fold in the cranberry sauce until evenly combined.
2. In a separate medium bowl with an electric hand mixer, whip together the heavy cream until stiff peaks form, 1 to 2 minutes. With a rubber spatula, fold the whipped cream into the cranberry-cream cheese mixture until evenly combined.
3. Fold in the pecans and mini marshmallows until evenly combined. Carefully fold in the mandarin oranges until evenly combined.
4. Transfer the cranberry-orange fluff to a serving bowl, wrap with plastic wrap, and chill in the refrigerator until ready to serve.

Note: The flavors will continue to develop the longer it chills; the best is overnight.

STRAWBERRY PRETZEL "SALAD"

FOR THE CRUST

2 cups (220 g) pretzels
3 tablespoons granulated sugar
½ cup (113 g) unsalted butter, melted

FOR THE CREAM CHEESE LAYER

One 8-ounce package cream cheese
1 cup (113 g) powdered sugar
1 teaspoon vanilla bean paste
1 cup (240 g) heavy whipping cream

FOR THE STRAWBERRY LAYER

Two 3-ounce packages strawberry powdered gelatin mix
2 cups (480 g) boiling water
1 pound strawberries, hulled and chopped

At a housewarming party, I was thrilled to see a strawberry pretzel pie on the dessert table, but the host quickly corrected me, saying, "We call that strawberry pretzel salad down here, honey." I chuckled, thinking there was nothing "salad" about this dessert, but I've come to appreciate the charming name.

However, I have yet to grow to love the dessert's fragile crust, typically prepared in a shallow rectangular pan with no border to hold in the creamy center or withstand the weight of the gelatin topping. So, to counter these structural challenges, I've adapted the recipe. Prepared in a springform pan, the crust amount is doubled to make a ¼-inch-thick crust that comes up around the edges, creating a sturdier structure. It's the same dessert, just a little stronger, no matter what you prefer to call it.

1. Preheat your oven to 400°F and set aside a 10-inch springform pan.
2. Prepare the crust. In a food processor, pulse the pretzels until finely crushed into crumbs.
3. In a small bowl, add the pretzel crumbs and sugar and whisk until evenly combined. Add the butter and with a fork, mix together until evenly combined and the mixture looks like wet beach sand.
4. Using the bottom of a 1-cup measuring cup, press the mixture into the bottom of the springform pan. Bake for 10 minutes. Place on a wire rack and cool completely.

continues

5 Meanwhile, prepare the cream cheese layer. In a medium bowl with an electric hand mixer, cream together the cream cheese, powdered sugar, and vanilla bean paste until light and fluffy, 2 to 3 minutes. Set aside.

6 In a separate medium bowl with an electric hand mixer, whip the heavy cream until stiff peaks form, 1 to 2 minutes. With a rubber spatula, fold the whipped cream into the cream cheese mixture until evenly combined. Pour the mixture into the cooled crust and chill in the refrigerator for at least 30 minutes.

7 Meanwhile, prepare the strawberry layer. In a medium heatproof bowl, whisk together the strawberry powdered gelatin and boiling water until evenly combined and the mix is dissolved. Chill in the refrigerator for about 30 minutes so the mixture can cool.

8 Once cooled, spread the strawberries over the cream cheese layer evenly. Carefully and slowly, pour the gelatin mixture over the strawberries. Stop when the mixture reaches the top edges of the crust (you don't want the gelatin to overflow; this would cause the crust and gelatin to stick to the pan). If foam appears on top of the gelatin, use a spoon and gently remove the foam. Chill in the refrigerator for at least 4 hours, best overnight, before serving.

I FOUND FAMILY AND ACCEPTANCE

WHEN YOU walk into our house, there's a good chance you'll be greeted by our little DJ, most likely playing Whitney Houston's "I Wanna Dance with Somebody" on repeat. You might catch a snippet of Miley Cyrus's "Doctor (Work It Out)" with some impromptu music video choreography. Depending on the day, Daft Punk might make an appearance, too.

As for me, I'm usually bouncing between baking in the kitchen, jotting down recipe notes or the stories behind them, and doing laundry, with occasional garden check-ins. Meanwhile, Louis is already planning dinner at 10 AM, thinking about home improvements, and sending me links to houses he's found for inspiration. In his downtime, he's either playing with our son, sending me Instagram memes, or chatting with his parents.

Our three dogs each have their quirks. Booker is usually outside, chasing neighborhood cats. Winnie is our little sweetheart, keeping the dog beds warm by switching between them. And Lenox? Lenox loves to drink water and then track it through the house.

Is this the life I imagined? It's more than I ever dreamed of. It's chaotic, simple, homey, and sometimes exhausting. But it's everything I could ever want. We juggle work and family, daydream about the future, and reminisce, holding on to those memories dearly.

I've found fulfillment and success in this life. I'm comfortable in my skin, in control of my thoughts, confident in my choices, open to change, and at peace. The journey here was challenging, but it's a story I'm proud to share. I spent 40 years seeking, experiencing, redirecting, and finding the pieces that fit me.

Louis and I work in sync in the kitchen, with our backs bumping because it's too small for two. He cooks while I bake, as we share the same goal: to provide for our family.

We're modern but rooted in family values, creating an environment where Jasper can build memories that will guide him. We want to show him that blood and chosen families are important and that they can intertwine to create a strong bond and community.

This life we've built is more than I ever imagined, and I wouldn't change a thing.

ACKNOWL

Javier, should these words find their way to you, and should you recognize the echoes of a younger Justin within these pages after two decades, I hope you know how grateful I am for you. The passing of time may have led us to lose touch in an era before social media, but your impact on my life remains unforgettable. I sincerely hope life has treated you kindly. Thank you for your kindness, support, and generosity in welcoming me into your world and opening the door to a place I feared but desperately wanted to enter. You were right; it's a beautiful world with endless possibilities and unconditional love.

My dearest best friend, Kristy, I don't even know where to begin. Our friendship is a rarity, having known each other since preschool. Your companionship is a treasure, a rare and invaluable bond that has withstood time. I cannot fathom traversing life's journey without you by my side. You, who knows me best, have been my unwavering constant. We have met life head-on together for over 35 years and have seen each other in multiple seasons. Thank you for your patience, unconditional loyalty, and ability to champion me with your delicate words and indestructible love. I love you so much; your friendship has saved me more than you know.

Ali, I can't imagine writing this cookbook without your love and support. You are a steadfast companion and confidant. Your loyalty and boundless support have been indispensable on this journey. I can't explain your importance; you have stood by my side, providing a sanctuary to unravel and the strength to rebuild. As my sister, uninhibited confidant, and cherished friend, you have been the driving force behind the transformation of audacious dreams into a vibrant and fulfilling reality. I love you and will always return the gracious support you have provided.

Michael, thank you for the countless things you have done for me and continue to do. You remind me regularly that I've earned this, that I've worked hard, and that I'm good enough. I am so grateful for your friendship. You are someone who challenges my thinking and pushes me toward growth and reflection. I cannot thank you enough for what you have generously done and continue to do for me. I hope I can return the favor one day.

EDGMENTS

Sally, my incredible, hardworking, best-of-the-best agent, I don't even know where to begin. I wouldn't have written this book if you hadn't seen something in me and the stories and recipes I wanted to share. You believed in me, championed me, and showed me that there are publications out there that believe queer voices deserve a place to share their experiences and document their history. Writing this book has been a personal journey, and your patience with me has been invaluable. You are incredible, and I am so lucky to have you as my agent. Thank you for believing in me and pushing me to pursue this dream.

Ann and Allison, you have been a complete joy to work with! This journey has been a dream of mine for so long, and you made the process an unbelievable experience. Ann, you have been the best editor I have worked with, and I am so grateful for your insight and ability to push my writing to a new level. Allison, your enthusiasm for this book and immediate understanding of my vision made this experience unforgettable. You both understood my point of view and vision, you championed these stories, and you made sure this book represented the queer community first and foremost. Thank you for allowing me this opportunity to contribute to the ongoing efforts of bringing more queer narratives forward, especially in food.

Brian and Catrine, this book is about precisely what happened when shooting the photographs for it. We were strangers who came together, quickly became friends, and forged a bond. What a magical experience we share!

Brian, I am so honored you photographed this book. When I knew this book would be published, you were the only photographer I wanted on the project. I cannot think of anyone else who could have achieved the look and feel of this book. You brought the emotion of the book to life. You captured the meaning of why we bring people together centered around food in our community. I am over the moon with how this book includes you and your personal touch. I am so grateful our working relationship turned into friendship. Thank you for being part of this and becoming a friend, which has enriched my life.

Catrine, without you this book would have been just another cookbook filled with pictures of food. Instead, your unmatched creativity infused life and motion into each photo, connecting a cohesive story. Having been a fan of your styling capabilities for so many years, I was thrilled to have you be part of this. More important, I am so grateful that you opened your home to shoot the dishes and welcomed me into your world with open arms. The creation of this book will always be a memory I cherish, but it is the time you, Brian, and I spent between shots and after a long day that I will hold closest to my heart. I am honored to call you a friend and share this book with you.

James, I don't even know where to start. Part of writing this cookbook was allowing myself to fully acknowledge and accept myself for me, to be unapologetic, and to live outwardly how I felt inward. Having you alongside me, you guided me through a transformative time, being a creative peer, understanding where my fears come from, and providing the tools needed to face life in style. You have indeed become a friend, and I am forever grateful that I can confidently walk into a room and show up for myself and our community. It's all thanks to you!

I wish I could individually thank every single person I've come to love and consider part of my chosen family. Every one of you have played a significant role in my life, showing up when I needed you the most, whether I knew it or not at the time. You've given me so much to be thankful for, be it patience, love, adventure, advice, and, most important, a space for respite and restoration. I love you all so much, and even though our lives have taken us in different directions in time, the memories we created and lessons we taught each other stay with me every day.

In heartfelt acknowledgment, I extend my gratitude to Booker, Winnie, Lenox, and Wrigley. Your unwavering reminders to take breaks during writing inertia or kitchen conundrums have been invaluable. Special thanks for your steadfast commitment to tidying up fallen scraps and stray splatters of batter—truly the best cleanup crew. You four-legged companions are simply the best dogs.

I want to express my heartfelt gratitude to Nancy, Lou Lou, and Lauren for their immediate warm embrace and acceptance of both me and Jasper into their family. The familial bond we share goes beyond mere in-laws; it fulfills a longing I've carried for 35 years. Your exemplary display of family support, unconditional love, and unwavering loyalty has not only healed my heart but has also satisfied my childhood yearning for unconditional love, acceptance, and fearless championing. With you as grandparents and an aunt to Jasper, he couldn't be in better hands. Your interest in and support during this cookbook journey mean more to me than words can convey. I sincerely hope that the final product was worth the wait and that it makes you proud. I love you!

My dear, sweet Jasper. I wish I could come up with the right words to explain how much I love you. From the very first moment I held you, you stole my heart. Thank you for being my baking buddy and always wanting to stand beside me in the kitchen and learn. Thank you for keeping me smiling and laughing during the most challenging moments writing this book and for making me stop and listen to Whitney and dance it out. Your support and patience during this were remarkable; you are so caring and wise beyond your years. I love you, and this book is for you to know who your families are.

Louis, my husband, thank you! You deserve a medal for the husband of the century for putting up with me during this. The sheer panic that would hit, the emotional and mental process of unpacking endless stories of my past to put into this book, put me in a series of moods that were challenging to cope with. But you were patient and kind, and generously let me work it out knowing in the end it would be worth it and that I would be a better human for it. You have pushed me in new directions, steering my fears into fuel, breaking down walls I have built, and planted the seed to believe in myself confidently. Your lack of hesitation to support, your willingness to get your hands dirty, and your time spent pushing me are a whole new level of support and love. Thank you for allowing my dreams and wild ambitions to happen; you never say no but instead let's make it happen. You are my best friend, and I love you. Thank you for loving me for who I am. This book is as much yours as it is mine: for the hours, the baking assistance, and the endless eating of desserts for months. I can't imagine life without you and look forward to the future we're building for us, Jasper, and our community. I promise, there's a big vacation in your future!

INDEX

D

E

F

G